A Bibliography on
Historical Organization Practices

Interpretation

Compiled by
Rosemary S. Reese

Edited by
Frederick L. Rath, Jr.
and
Merrilyn Rogers O'Connell

American Association for State and Local History
Nashville, Tennessee

We are grateful for the generous support of the American Conservation Association, Inc. for their assistance in the publication of this volume

Publication of this book was made possible in part by funds from the sale of the Bicentennial State Histories

Library of Congress Cataloging in Publication Data Revised

Rath, Frederick L
  A bibliography on historical organization practices.

  Includes indexes.
  CONTENTS: v. 1. Historic preservation.
          —v. 3. Reese, R.S. Interpretation.
  1. Historic buildings—United States—Conservation
and restoration—Bibliography.   2. Historic sites—
United States—Conservation and restoration—Bibliography.   3. Historic buildings—Conservation and restoration—Bibliography.   4. Historical museums—Bibliography.   5. Museum techniques—Bibliography.
I. O'Connell, Merrilyn Rogers, joint author.
II. Reese, Rosemary S., joint author.   III. Title.
Z1251,A2R35 [E159]   016.973   75–26770

Printed in the United States of America

Interpretation

Contents

6. Museum Exhibits   46

7. Museums in the Media Age   61

Appendix: Periodicals Cited   71

Index   75

Preface

In 1970 the American Association of Museums Committee on Accreditation formulated the following official definition of a museum:

> An organized and permanent nonprofit institution, essentially educational or aesthetic in purpose, with professional staff, which owns and utilizes tangible objects, cares for them, and exhibits them to the public on some regular schedule.

This understanding of museums as educational institutions is a relatively new development. Nineteenth-century museums provided open storage exhibits, an occasional Sunday lecture and little more. Museums were not generally recognized as educational institutions but merely as repositories for the accumulation of the ages. However, with the increased visitation made possible by the automobile and the shorter work week, and with the increasing involvement of taxpayers' dollars in the support of museums, the obligation to be educational institutions has become very important. Today the role of the museum as an educational institution is not only acknowledged but assumed as one of its principal functions, second only to its preservation/conservation responsibilities. The way in which a museum uses its resources to carry out its educational function is "Interpretation," the subject of the third volume of the *Bibliography on Historical Organization Practices*.

For historical organizations, interpretation has a special meaning. It is based on a gathering of facts, a trick (an art, if you wish) that can be learned by any competent scholar. But the past will still elude us if facts are all that have been found. Museums, however, deal with objects and images, many of which have a strong appeal to a public that has little background for understanding them. The objects, the images, even the documents at times must be interpreted—that is, there must be an attempt to make them understood. History museums and historic sites, then, are in the business of raising consciousness. It is their mission to reveal in such a way that visitors will think for themselves not about the facts, which are inert, but about the meanings, the ideas, the relationships and the concepts that derive from the facts.

So the task of interpretation is a large one. Every year millions of Americans visit hundreds of historical societies, historic sites, and museums throughout the country. They come from many places and for many reasons. A few are serious scholars pursuing specific areas of interest. For them the museum or historical society as a research facility is paramount. Far outnumbering the scholars, however, are those who are interested in learning something about their past, in a more general way. For these people the museum offers exhibits, adult education programs, walking tours, travelling museums, and community programs. In addition, thousands of school children visit museums each year as part of their regular course of study. For them museums must provide junior membership programs, children's museums, specially designed curriculum-oriented programs and audiovisual materials. All of these activities are the means through which interpretation is carried out.

This volume is designed to help anyone involved in the myriad of educational activities conducted by historical organizations. This includes education department staff, docents and guides, both paid and volunteer, historic site interpreters, children's museum staff, junior program sponsors, teachers, exhibit designers and technicians, and audiovisual specialists.

Like the editions which preceded it, this bibliography is selective rather than definitive. It seeks to include all the most significant references, but some older materials, particularly periodical literature, and some superseded materials have been dropped in order to accommodate the burgeoning new literature. The compilers, aided by their expert advisors, have also exercised an arbitrary discretion in not listing articles in obscure or unobtainable editions or periodicals. Although some early seminal or definitive references are still included, the concentration is on books and pamphlets, and articles published since 1945.

As in the second edition, all entries for books and pamphlets follow the Library of Congress main entry headings and have additional data based on the Library of Congress catalog card information. Thus, all include the following: number of pages or number of volumes; illustrations (drawings, plans, photographs, or other graphic materials); bibliography or bibliographical notes (if any).

The primary purpose of the bibliography is to be a working tool, providing the first steps on research trails or program planning. To add to its practicality, the compilers have included annotations where the title of the book or article does not give a clear idea of subject matter. They have included filmed and taped materials where appropriate. At the end of many chapters there are notes on periodicals, organizations or services. The appendix lists all periodicals from which articles have been cited, with addresses and subscription information. The index, derived from a punch card retrieval system, is deliberately comprehensive, so that the most obscure references, coauthors, and editors can be tracked down easily.

There are two other departures from what may be considered standard bibliographical practice which seek to give further dimension to the usefulness of the work. A Basic Reference Shelf, thoroughly annotated, is offered in order to give immediate practical guidance on the many facets of interpretation. There is also a discursive section on major historical organizations, national, foreign, and international. In addition, there are cross-references and notations, where appropriate, to the preceding volumes in the *Bibliography* series.

To produce a work of this kind, the help of many individuals and organizations is necessary. Rosemary S. Reese, associate editor of the Bibliographic Project, served as principal compiler of this volume. The Smithsonian Institution, as administrator of National Museum Act funds, made the expanded Bibliographic Project possible; we are especially grateful to the Advisory Council and to Paul N. Perrot for their interest and support. The New York State Historical Association provided not only rooms for the small staff but also the full services of its fine library.

In compiling this volume, *Interpretation,* several individuals served as able, cheerful, and unpaid reviewers of the materials in their specialities: Richard S. Allen, New York State American Revolution Bicentennial Commission; Ann Bay, Office of Elementary and Secondary Education, Smithsonian Institution; Shirley P. Low, formerly of Colonial Williamsburg; Arminta Neal, Denver Museum of Natural History; Doris Platt, State Historical Society of Wisconsin; and Milo V. Stewart, New York State Historical Association.

As we noted in the first two volumes, the American Association for State and Local History undertook the support of the Bibliographic Project in recognition of the need for a reference guide to the literature produced by and for a rapidly growing profession. We are indebted to the Association's director, Dr. William T. Alderson, for his continuing guidance in this effort, and to the Association's publications department, directed by Gary Gore, for supervising the production of these volumes.

May the references and notes contained herein be useful, practical, and inspirational in your interpretation programs.

Frederick L. Rath, Jr.
*Deputy Commissioner for Historic
Preservation, New York State
Office of Parks and Recreation*

Merrilyn Rogers O'Connell
Director, Bibliographic Project

A Bibliography on Historical
Organization Practices

Interpretation

Basic Reference Shelf

Selected from the six major subject areas of interpretation is a Basic Reference Shelf of monographs, reports, handbooks, and conference papers that should provide staff members, interpreters, teachers, and exhibit planners with a working library. Ranging from education program surveys to audiovisual techniques, the following annotated references contain bibliographies, source lists, project abstracts, and how-to-do-it materials.

Also recommended is membership in one or more major historical organizations, and/or subscription to specialized journals in order to keep up with recent trends, new materials, and important publications.

Alderson, William T., and Shirley P. Low. *Interpretation of Historic Sites.* Nashville, Tenn.: American Association for State and Local History, 1976. 189 pp., illus., bibliog., appendices, index. ◆ Considers the practical problems of developing and conducting interpretive programs, from setting objectives through evaluation of the established program.

America the Beautiful Fund. *Old Glory: A Pictorial Report on the Grass Roots History Movement and the First Hometown History Primer.* New York: Warner Publishing Co., 1973. 191 pp., illus. ◆ Descriptions of America the Beautiful Fund Projects.

American Association of Museums. *Museums: Their New Audience.* A Report to the Department of Housing and Urban Development by a Special Committee of the American Association of Museums. Washington, D.C.: American Association of Museums, 1972. 108 pp., illus., diagrams, bibliog.

American Revolution Bicentennial Administration. *Official Master Reference for Bicentennial Activities.* 2nd ed. Washington, D.C.: American Revolution Bicentennial Administration, 1974. 294 pp. ◆ To be revised and updated four times a year. Contains indexes and abstracts of Bicentennial Projects catalogued in the ARBA Bicentennial Information Network (Binet), a computerized information system. Printouts are available at a minimum charge of $15.00.

Bay, Ann. *Museum Programs for Young People.* Washington, D.C.: Smithsonian Institution, 1973. 282 pp., illus. ◆ Case studies of education programs in fourteen American museums and discussion of programs of special interest. Includes information on exhibits, in-museum programs, extension services, staff, funding, coordination with schools, facilities and publications.

Bloomberg, Marguerite. *An Experiment in Museum Instruction . . . Conducted at the Cleveland Museum of Art to Determine the Relative Effectiveness of Several Types of Museum Lessons for Children of Average and High Mentality.* Washington, D.C.: American Association of Museums, 1929. 40 pp., illus. ◆ Photocopy available from ERIC Document Reproduction Service, Computer Microfilm International Corporation, P.O. Box 190, Arlington, Virginia 22210. ERIC # ED 044 921. The study is a comparison of the educational effectiveness of a variety of learning strategies in the Cleveland Museum of Art for groups of students ranked by their schools into different ability groups. It is a classical experimental study on varying methods of museum school tour instruction and arousing exploration behavior in children.

Bruner, Jerome S. *The Process of Education.* Cambridge, Mass.: Harvard University Press, 1960. 97 pp. ♦ Thoughts growing out of a conference of scientists, scholars, and educators in 1959, discussing how science education might be improved in U.S. elementary and secondary schools.

Cook, Anne H., and Jane T. Breinholt. *Project 1776: A Manual for the Bicentennial.* Rev. ed. Devon, Pa.: Pennsylvania Bicentennial Commission, 1974. 206 pp., illus., bibliog. ♦ A source book of history and learning ideas in Early American Culture for elementary school pupils.

Dale, Edgar. *Audiovisual Methods in Teaching.* 3rd ed. New York: Dryden Press, 1969. 719 pp., illus., bibliog., sources of teaching materials.

International Council of Museums. *Museums and Young People.* Paris: International Council of Museums, 1952. 131 pp. ♦ Articles by Germain Cart, Molly Harrison, and Charles Russell. Available from ERIC Document Reproduction Service, Computer Microfilm International Corporation, P.O. Box 190, Arlington, Virginia 22210. ERIC # ED 046 233.

Kemp, Jerrold E., et al. *Planning and Producing Audiovisual Materials.* 2nd ed. San Francisco: Chandler Publishing Co., 1968. 251 pp., illus., bibliog. ♦ Includes planning audiovisual materials, fundamental skills (photography, graphics, sound recording), and producing materials (picture series, slides, filmstrips, transparencies, motion pictures, television).

Neal, Arminta. *Exhibits for the Small Museum: A Handbook.* With an Introductory Essay by H. J. Swinney. Nashville, Tenn.: American Association for State and Local History, 1976. 169 pp., photos, diagrams, appendices. ♦ This how-to-do-it manual discusses case exhibit design and installation, lighting, labels, mannikins, scale models, and adaptation of old buildings for exhibit purposes. Since this very useful publication is a continuation and expansion of *Help! For the Small Museum* by the same author, it has been included although published after the closing date for compilation.

Neal, Arminta. *Help! For the Small Museum; A Handbook of Exhibit Ideas and Methods.* Boulder, Colo.: Pruett Publishing, 1969. 200 pp., photos, drawings, diagrams, sources of supply, bibliog. ♦ Covers general principles, planning, design of exhibits, labels, color and light, case exhibits, construction notes, tools, and materials.

Nicol, Elizabeth H. *The Development of Validated Museum Exhibits.* Washington, D.C.: U.S. Department of Health, Education and Welfare, Office of Education, Bureau of Research, 1969. 114 pp. ♦ Available from ERIC Document Reproduction Service, Computer Microfilm International Corporation, P.O. Box 190, Arlington, Virginia 22210. ERIC # ED 035 038. Discusses the museum as a learning environment. Exhibit development is treated as an evolutionary process, drawing the museum visitor into the collaborative venture of testing and improving the exhibits.

Rogers, Lola Erikson. *Museums and Related Institutions; A Basic Program Survey.* Washington, D.C.: U.S. Office of Education, 1969. 120 pp., illus., graphs, tables. ♦ Based upon a pioneering survey of 2889 establishments considered to conform to a working definition of museum, this study was undertaken for the U.S. Office of Education in cooperation with the Smithsonian Institution and the American Association of Museums. It provides important overall information on governing authority, type of exhibits, location by city and state, paid and volunteer staff, study facilities, level of operating expenditure, number of annual visits, and educational services.

Smithsonian Institution Conference on Museums and Education, University of Vermont, 1966. *Museums and Education: Papers.* Edited by Eric Larrabee. Washington, D.C.: Smithsonian Institution Press, 1968. 255 pp., bibliog. ♦ Contains some thought-provoking essays on museum education, its current status, its techniques, its function in various kinds of museums and its prospects for the future.

Tilden, Freeman. *Interpreting Our Heritage.* Rev. ed. Chapel Hill, N.C.: University of North Carolina Press, 1967. 120 pp., illus. ♦ Develops a philosophy of interpretation which points up the need to involve visitors in the interpretation and to make sites meaningful for them.

Wasserman, Paul, ed. *Museum Media: A Biennial Directory and Index of Publications*

2

and *Audiovisuals Available from United States and Canadian Institutions.* Detroit: Gale Research Co., 1973. 455 pp. ◆ Intended to provide bibliographic control of books, booklets, and monographs, catalogs, pamphlets and leaflets, films and filmstrips, and other media which are prepared and distributed by museums, art galleries and related institutions in the United States and Canada. Biennial publication is planned.

Zetterberg, Hans L. *Museums and Adult Education.* New York: A. M. Kelley for the International Council of Museums, 1969. 89 pp., illus., bibliog. ◆ A comprehensive discussion of the role of museums in adult education. Sponsored by the ICOM Committee for Education and Cultural Action with the assistance of UNESCO.

1
Historical Organizations

Historical organizations, both national and international, provide an important communication network of what is going on in the field of interpretation. They are clearinghouses of information, publishers of books and newsletters, sponsors of meetings and seminars, and promoters of new materials and techniques to improve the quality of education programs.

Listed in the following chapter are the major national and international agencies with a statement of their purposes and activities, and descriptions of the programs and publications that benefit those in the field. Specialized organizations are noted at the end of the appropriate chapters or subchapters.

National Organizations

American Association for State and Local History (AASLH), 1400 Eighth Avenue South, Nashville, Tennessee 37203.

The American Association for State and Local History, founded in 1940, is a nonprofit educational organization dedicated to advancing knowledge, understanding, and appreciation of localized history in the United States and Canada. It serves amateur and professional historians, individuals and organizations, and includes in its broad spectrum such groups as historical museums and libraries, junior history clubs, historic sites, manuscript collections, and large as well as small historical societies.

To encourage the development of popular knowledge about American history, the Association launched the magazine *American Heritage* in 1949. Within five years it became a bimonthly, hardcover magazine published professionally by American Heritage Publishing Company and cosponsored by the Association. Royalties help provide some of the financial resources needed to carry out the Association's broad educational and professional programs. In recent years, the National Endowment for the Humanities, the National Endowment for the Arts, the Council on Library Resources, and the National Museum Act have provided funds to the Association to support special training programs, seminars for historical agency personnel, consultant services, and publications.

Membership in the Association is open to professionals, institutions, libraries, and individuals.

PROFESSIONAL SERVICES: Clearinghouse for inquiries from individuals and organizations; cassette lectures and slide/tape training kits; research surveys about the profession;

job placement service; consultant service to historical societies and museums; annual awards of merit and commendation for outstanding contributions to the field by individuals and organizations; cooperative programs with state and regional conferences of historical organizations; annual meeting; joint meetings with related historical organizations.

PUBLICATIONS: *History News,* monthly magazine of up-to-date news of members, events, new ideas, reviews of books, and a Technical Leaflet series of how-to-do-it articles (with a 3-ring binder, available); *Directory of Historical Societies and Agencies in the United States and Canada,* biennial; Bicentennial State Histories series; books and booklets; job placement newsletter, quarterly; *Newsletter,* occasional, special issues on matters of urgent importance; catalog of Association publications and technical leaflets; catalog of slide/tape training kits and cassette lectures. *History News* and out-of-print volumes of Association *Bulletins,* a series of booklets published between 1941 and 1973 which preceded the Technical Leaflet series, are available in microfilm from Xerox University Microfilms, 300 N. Zeeb Road, Ann Arbor, Michigan 48106.

TRAINING PROGRAMS: Cosponsor of annual Williamsburg Seminar for Historical Administrators; seminars on publications, administration of historical agencies and museums, historical museum techniques, management and interpretation of history museums and historic sites; training seminars and regional workshops for beginning professionals and small agency directors.

American Association of Museums (AAM), 1055 Thomas Jefferson Street, N.W., Washington D.C. 20007.

Organized in 1906, the American Association of Museums is a nonprofit service organization that promotes museums as major cultural resources and represents the interests of the museum profession on a national level. The Association is supported primarily by dues and contributions from its membership, which includes museums of every size and discipline, museum employees and others concerned with the future of museums. Membership benefits include subscriptions to publications, services of the Professional Relations Committee, and use of the placement service.

The Association functions with administrative committees and special committees, including AAM/ICOM Committee, and Accreditation Commission; Advisors to the AAM Council; and Standing Professional Committees for Curators, Educators, Trustees, and Security.

REGIONAL GROUPS: A network of six regional affiliate groups helps to disperse information about museums and encourages cooperation among institutions, museum professionals, and the general public. Yearly meetings for members are sponsored in each of the regional conferences, and all publish a newsletter. The regions are: New England Conference (*NEC News*); Northeast Museums Conference (*The Museologist*); Midwest Museums Conference (*Midwest Museums Quarterly*): Mountain-Plains Museums Conference (*Mountain-Plains Museums Conference Newsletter*); Western Regional Conference (*WRC Newsletter*); Southeastern Museums Conference (*SEMC Notes; Inside SEMC*).

PROGRAMS: Professional Relations Service provides formal, objective third-party inquiry and reporting in employment disputes. Service is available only to voting members who file a formal request. Placement Service provides timely information on employment opportunities within the museum profession. The service is available to members and consists of advertisements of institutional positions open and individuals seeking employment in *AVISO,* the monthly newsletter. Accreditation sets prescribed professional criteria by which a museum's quality and performance may be judged. Accreditation certifies that a museum currently meets accepted standards established by the profession, but does not grade achievement or excellence beyond established minimum requirements. The program is administered by a seven-member commission that is representative of a range of geographic areas and professional disciplines. Travel Programs are arranged for groups of Association members. Special charter flights are planned for attendance at international events of special importance to the museum profession. Tours are also arranged in conjunction with AAM annual meetings. The Association sponsors special seminars in conjunction with regional conferences; and holds an annual meeting.

TRUSTEES COMMITTEE: The Museum Trustees Committee helps trustees fulfill their vital responsibilities to museums. It provides a forum for communication about federal and state programs, legislation and tax concerns, museum accreditation, sources of funding, and the preservation of our cultural and educational heritage. AAM trustee members receive all the benefits of individual membership, as well as a special quarterly newsletter directed to trustee interests. They may attend seminars for trustees on taxes, trustee responsibilities, finances, legislation and other topics pertaining to the trustee's role. Trustees are encouraged to attend AAM annual meetings and regional conferences. The Association offers special liability insurance for trustees.

PUBLICATIONS: *Museum News,* bimonthly journal on a range of subjects, special features and theme sections; *AVISO,* monthly newsletter, including current issues, "Washington Report," Placement Service, classified listings, and news of regional conferences and AAM professional committees (succeeds *AAM Bulletin*); *Official Museum Directory,* biennial; books, major reports, reprints of Technical Supplements and special articles (brochure available).

AAM/ICOM: In June 1973, with the merger of the U.S. National Committee of the International Council of Museums (ICOM) and the AAM, the U.S. Committee became an integral part of the Association as the AAM/ICOM Committee. Through this committee the Association participates in international museum activities. AAM members may join AAM/ICOM and receive such benefits as the *AAM/ICOM Newsletter;* the Paris-published quarterly magazine *ICOM News;* a membership card honored for free or reduced admission at many museums in Europe and the U.S.; use of the ICOM Documentation Centre in Paris; help in planning museum trips abroad; invitations to attend ICOM international meetings and the Triennial World Conference; and a discount on subscriptions to *Museum,* UNESCO's quarterly magazine. The AAM/ICOM office also sponsors, with the cooperation of the U.S. Department of State, annual visits to the United States by museum professionals from other countries.

National Trust for Historic Preservation (NTHP), 740-748 Jackson Place, N.W., Washington, D.C. 20006.

The National Trust for Historic Preservation was chartered by Congress in 1949 "to further the national policy of preserving for public use America's heritage of historic districts, sites, buildings, structures and objects; to facilitate public participation in the historic preservation movement and to serve that movement through educational and advisory programs; and to accept and administer for public benefit and use significant historic properties."

Membership in the National Trust is open to individuals, organizations, and businesses interested in historic preservation. Programs are supported by membership dues, endowment funds, contributions, and matching grants from the U.S. Department of the Interior, National Park Service, under provisions of the National Historic Preservation Act of 1966.

Programs are carried out under seven departments: Office of the President, Finance, Preservation Services, Historic Properties, Real Estate and Legal Services, Public Affairs, The Preservation Press. Advisory services are provided to preservation groups, community leaders, and city planning officials, and special liaison is maintained with federal programs. The National Trust is also in contact with numerous related groups, both national and international, concerned with architecture, urban history, landscape architecture, and other special interests. Information on preservation legislation, architectural surveys, and preservation projects is distributed throughout the country.

Field services are provided through five regional offices: Midwest Regional Office, 407 South Dearborn Street, Suite 710, Chicago, Illinois 60605; Western Regional Office, 802 Montgomery Street, San Francisco, California 94133; New England Field Service Office, 141 Cambridge Street, Boston, Massachusetts 02114 (sponsored jointly with the Society for the Preservation of New England Antiquities); Southwest/Plains Field Office, 903 Colcord Building, Oklahoma City, Oklahoma 73102; and, Mid-Atlantic Field Office, 1001 Connecticut Avenue, N.W., Suite 819, Washington, D.C. 20006.

PROFESSIONAL SERVICES: Clearinghouse of current information on preservation theories, techniques, standards, legislation; advisory services and visits by professional staff and consultants; lectures and visual aid materials; preservation archives and library; annual meeting and preservation conference; consultant service grants and National Historic Preservation Fund (brochure available); tours in the U.S. and abroad.

PUBLICATIONS (The Preservation Press): *Preservation News,* monthly newspaper of preservation activities, also available in xerographic print and microfilm from Xerox University Microfilms, 300 N. Zeeb Road, Ann Arbor, Michigan 48106; *Historic Preservation,* illustrated quarterly journal; *Member Organizations and Their Properties,* annual directory; *Annual Report;* Consultant Service Grant reports; conference proceedings, leaflet series; Trust property brochures. The Preservation Bookstore is located at National Trust headquarters and a catalogue is available.

EDUCATION PROGRAMS: Cosponsor of annual Williamsburg Seminar for Historical Administrators; annual Woodlawn Conference for Historical Museum Associates; technical conferences and seminars; youth work-study programs.

SPECIAL PROGRAMS: Special events and activities; awards; Employment Opportunities clearinghouse, WORK, a monthly column in *Preservation News*.

NATIONAL TRUST MUSEUMS: Belle Grove, (Va.), Chesterwood (Mass.), Cliveden (Pa.), Decatur House (D.C.), Lyndhurst (N.Y.), Oatlands (Va.), Shadows-on-the-Teche (La.), Woodlawn Plantation (Va.), Woodrow Wilson House (D.C.), descriptive brochures available. Eleven historic properties: Andalusia (Pa.), Batchelor's Hope (Md.), Bowlingly (Md.), Casa Amesti (Calif.), Cooper-Molera Adobe (Calif.), Drayton Hall (S.C.), Filoli (Calif.), Frank Lloyd Wright Home and Studio (Ill.), Mount Harmon Plantation (Md.), The Pope-Leighey House (Va.), Reynolds Tavern (Md.).

U.S. National Park Service (NPS), Department of the Interior, Washington, D.C. 20240

The National Park Service was created as a bureau of the Department of the Interior by Congress in 1916 and was charged with the administration of the small number of existing national parks and monuments, including some archeological and historical areas. The Historic Sites Act of 1935 established "a national policy to preserve for public use, historic sites, buildings and objects of national significance for the inspiration and benefit of the people of the United States." With new powers and responsibilities, the National Park Service embarked on a national preservation program.

Added to this legislative lineage is the National Historic Preservation Act of 1966 which significantly broadened the scope of national preservation policy. Under this new authority, the National Register of Historic Places was greatly expanded, a national Advisory Council on Historic Preservation was appointed, and a system of matching grants-in-aid to the states and the National Trust for Historic Preservation was established. An Office of Archeology and Historic Preservation was organized in 1967 to manage the increased responsibilities.

NATIONAL PARK SYSTEM: The Park System is composed of natural, historical, and cultural areas, totaling 298 as of January 1, 1977. Field direction is provided through eight regional offices: New England Region, Boston; Northeast Region, Philadelphia; Southeast Region, Atlanta; Midwest Region, Omaha; Southwest Region, Santa Fe; Western Region, San Francisco; Pacific Northwest Region, Seattle; parks and memorials in Washington D.C. are administered by the Office of National Capital Parks. Functions of planning, design and construction of physical facilities in the parks are carried out by the Denver Service Center. Production of publications, museum exhibits, and audiovisual programs is carried out by the Harpers Ferry Center. Cooperative research programs are conducted in conjunction with several universities throughout the country.

PUBLICATIONS: The National Park Service publication program is as varied as the parks it serves, from archeological studies and architectural records to maps and posters. There is an informational folder published for most of the parks. Over one hundred of the parks have interpretive handbooks and folders, all reasonably priced and sold in the visitor centers. The program further serves the public with fishing, boating, and camping information booklets; and, with the Administrative Policy series, it opens to the public rules, regulations, and standards by which the parks are managed and maintained.

TRAINING CENTERS: The Albright Training Center, Grand Canyon National Park, Arizona, is maintained for orientation and skills training for all new employees; the Mather Training Center, Harpers Ferry, West Virginia, is maintained for teaching interpretive methods. There are also a number of short courses at both centers for new and experienced rangers and interpreters. The Park Service maintains career and seasonal employment services for the park system.

PARK PRACTICE PROGRAM: Begun in 1957, the Park Practice Program is a mutual program of service to park and recreation people, cosponsored by the National Conference on State Parks, National Recreation and Park Association, and the National Park Service. The Program is a series of publications for individuals and organizations concerned with parks, recreation, and conservation. It seeks to communicate interesting and high quality practical information on planning, designing, operating and administering recreation facilities. The publications are available through full membership or individual subscriptions. The Park Practice Program is located at the National Recreation and Park Association, 1601 North Kent Street, Arlington, Virginia 22209.

Grist—bimonthly, tested time-, effort-, and money–saving technical ideas and devices for more effective park operation; Guideline—bimonthly, members exchange methods of management, administration, and interpretation of park and recreation facilities; Trends—quarterly, features new and important issues relating to parks, recreation, and conservation; Design—semiannually, innovative structural designs and layout plans for work and recreation sites to better serve visitor needs; Plowback—discontinued.

EASTERN NATIONAL PARK AND MONUMENT ASSOCIATION: The Association is a private, nonprofit organization formed in 1948 to promote the historical, scientific, educational, and interpretive activities of the National Park Service, principally in the eastern half of the United States, through grants-in-aid for research, publication of historical literature, development of park libraries, acquisition of museum objects, subsidies for experimental interpretive techniques, and acquisition of lands needed to prevent intrusions on present areas. It is located at 311 Walnut Street, Philadelphia, Pennsylvania 19106. Its publications include: Newsletter, twice a year to members; Agency News, sent to agents five to seven times a year covering new sales facilities, sales techniques, changes in policies and personnel; Annual Report; publications for sale at National Park Service sites.

SOUTHWESTERN MONUMENTS ASSOCIATION: The Association is a nonprofit publishing and distributing organization supporting historical, scientific, and educational activities of the National Park Service. It was formed in 1946 to provide accurate information concerning the Southwest to the traveling public; to stimulate and encourage scientific research in the historical and natural sciences within the National Park System areas in the Southwest; to publish informational and technical papers dealing with various historical and natural sciences; to develop and maintain in the National Park Service areas reference libraries available to the public; and to assemble and safeguard in the National Park Service areas of the Southwest study collections and exhibits germane to these areas. The Association publishes a catalog listing items distributed through its sales centers.

ADMINISTRATION: Because of the expansion of nonpark programs such as the National Register, grants, surveys, and interagency services, the National Park Service reorganized its divisions in the historic preservation field into two major offices in 1973. Park Historic Preservation is responsible for programs within the parks; the Office of Archeology and Historic Preservation handles all nonpark programs. The Advisory Council on Historic Preservation was established as an independent federal agency in 1976 (P.L. 94-422).

Park Historic Preservation, under the reorganization of NPS historic preservation programs, combines the divisions for history, archeology, and architecture. The Division of History is responsible for the research and recommendations on all historical matters for the National Park Service. It does the basic research for the whole program of preservation and interpretation in all of the national park sites, and carries on annual research programs and individual studies. The Division of Archeology conducts archeological investigations in areas of the National Park System where prehistoric and historic people have lived. Its Archeological Research series is a program for the publication of information derived from archeological projects, and made available in the form of published reports for use in libraries and research institutions. The archeology program, begun in 1906 and expanded by the preservation legislation of 1935 and 1966, is served by the Southwest Archeological Center, Globe, Arizona, and the Southeast Archeological Center, Macon, Georgia. The Division of Architecture is responsible for the restoration of historic structures under the control of the National Park Service. It conducts all the research, planning, and execution of the restorations, and also conducts a training program to perpetuate the traditional building crafts necessary for truly accurate restorations.

The Office of Archeology and Historic Preservation was first organized in 1967 from existing professional staffs within the National Park Service. Its purpose was to carry out more fully the preservation policies of the federal acts of 1906, 1935, and 1966. In 1973 all nonpark programs in historic preservation were reorganized under the Office and included four main divisions: Division of the National Register, Division of Grants, Division of Historic and Architectural Surveys, Division of Interagency Services. These Divisions and their special programs and responsibilities are described in detail in Volume 1 of the *Bibliography . . . : Historic Preservation.*

Foreign and International Organizations

Canadian Museums Association (CMA), 331 Cooper Street, Suite 400, Ottawa, Ontario K2P 0G5.

The Canadian Museums Association was incorporated in 1947 to promote, on a national basis, the interests of all Canadian museums and the welfare of their staffs. Its purposes are to advance public museum and art gallery services in Canada by promoting among museums a greater consciousness of their responsibilities as cultural institutions; acting as a clearinghouse for information of special interest and relevance to the Canadian museum scene; promoting and supporting museum training programs; extending assistance to museums in securing competent staff; and cooperating with regional, national and international associations to serve better the museum community in Canada.

The Association is governed by a national council of sixteen members, elected by individual, institution and association members. The Executive Committee is composed of the President, Vice President, and Secretary-Treasurer, and is aided by committees on education, elections, finance, membership, publications, and training.

Membership includes the voting categories of individual, association and institution, and nonvoting categories of student and affiliate. The Association sponsors regional meetings and seminars, and holds an annual conference.

PUBLICATIONS: *CMA Gazette/AMC Gazette,* quarterly beginning Winter 1975 (succeeds bimonthly magazine published 1966-1974); *museogramme,* monthly, newsletter begun 1973 for members; *Basic Museum Management; The Technical Requirements of Small Museums;* annual report; conference proceedings; *Directory of Canadian Museums; CMA Bibliography.*

TRAINING RESOURCES PROGRAM: The Association has revised its correspondence course to serve as an introduction to basic museum principles and practice with certification being awarded upon successful completion; a resource center with a library and publications order service; and a resource services program to aid those involved in training programs that includes lists of instructors, a seminar procedures manual, and audiovisual training aids. The Program also has a national seminar program including seminars for professionals in addition to a special session at the annual conference; a training publications program including materials published in the quarterly or in separate pamphlets; and limited financial aid for special research projects and internships.

The Museums Association, 87 Charlotte Street, London W1P 2BX, England.

Founded in 1889, The Museums Association is an organization comprising and representing museums and art galleries and those who work in them both in the British Isles and overseas. The purposes of the Association are to promote the establishment and better administration of museums and art galleries and to improve the qualifications and status of members of museum staffs.

Its activities include the collection and publication of information about museums and the subjects they deal with, and the arrangement of courses of study in these subjects. The Association endeavors to represent the interests of museums and the profession in dealings with governmental and other outside bodies, whether public or private, national or foreign, and also to assist such bodies to establish a closer relationship with museums. It maintains links, in the interests of international cooperation, with related organizations in all parts of the world, including UNESCO and the International Council of Museums.

The Museums Association works in collaboration with the Carnegie United Kingdom Trust, which has made grants for the improvement of the museum service in the British Isles. Assistance from the Trust is available for the provision of expert reports on the development or reorganization of museums and art galleries, towards the provision of new facilities or projects in the museum field, including countryside schemes under the áegis of museums, and collaboration between museums. Grants are also available for training projects for students at the Leicester University Department of Museum Studies and other approved training bodies, and for study tours to enable members of museum staffs to gain experience relevant to their museum duties. In addition, the Trust makes a contribution towards the cost of the educational services provided by the Association.

Membership is open to persons connected with or interested in museums. There are eight classes of members including fellows, students, and institutions. The Association sponsors an annual five-day conference, and other meetings to promote exchange of information between members of museum staffs.

PUBLICATIONS: *Museums Journal,* quarterly, technical index for 1930-55 and 1955-66 available; *Bulletin,* monthly newsletter for members; *Museums Yearbook,* annual (succeeds *Calendar*), directory of museums and art galleries in the British Isles; Handbooks for Museum Curators series, published 1956-1967; Information Sheets series, begun 1967.

TRAINING PROGRAMS: The Diploma of the Association is the recognized qualification in curatorship within the museum profession, and is awarded on the recommendation of the Association's Education Committee to those members who have had at least three years' fulltime experience in a museum or art gallery (or two years, if university graduates), have completed the required courses of study, and have passed the prescribed examinations. By the institution of the Diploma, which is the essential qualification for Associateship, and by the election of suitably qualified Associates as Fellows, the Association endeavours to set standards of curatorship and professional ability that will be recognized both inside and outside the profession. A Conservation Certificate has been instituted for those museum staff whose work is primarily concerned with the conservation and restoration of museum objects. The Technical Certificate of the Association is the qualification for museum workers whose duties are primarily technical, and is awarded after examination to candidates who have not less than five years' experience in museum work.

SPECIAL GROUPS: Information Retrieval Group of the Museums Association, organized in 1968; Group for Education Services in Museums.

International Council of Museums (ICOM), 1 rue Miollis, 75732 Paris 15e, France.

Founded in 1946, the International Council of Museums is the international, nongovernmental, and professional organization representing museums and the museum profession. It maintains close consultative and cooperative relations with UNESCO, International Council of Monuments and Sites (ICOMOS), and the International Centre for the Study of the Preservation and the Restoration of Cultural Property (Rome Centre), and other national, regional, or international, intergovernmental or nongovermental organizations, with the authorities responsible for museums and with specialists of other disciplines. The primary aims are: to define, support and aid museums and the museum institution; to establish, support, and reinforce the museum profession; to organize cooperation and mutual assistance between museums and between the members of the museum profession in the different countries; to emphasize the importance of the role played by museums and the museum profession within each community and in the promotion of a greater knowledge and understanding among peoples.

The General Assembly is the governing body of ICOM. Activities are carried out through the Paris-based Secretariat, National Committees, and International Committees. The Secretariat conducts the day-to-day operation of the organization and world-wide coordination of its activities and programs. Through its National Committees ICOM coordinates a vast international effort between all countries aimed at a thorough and progressive transformation of the concept of a museum; toward an increase of its scientific role; improvements in display and exhibition; the modernization and expansion of its educational and cultural activities; and the preservation of the cultural heritage through conservation.

The International Committees are composed of the leading authorities in a given type of museum discipline, or in an activity common to all museums. These groups of professionals come together regularly to discuss latest developments, familiarize themselves with new techniques, and make recommendations which serve the interest of ICOM members throughout the world. The Committees are: Archaeology and History; Architecture and Museum Techniques; Applied Art; Modern Art; Conservation; Costume; Documentation; Education; Ethnography; International Art Exhibitions; Training of Personnel; Musical Instruments (CIMCIM); Regional Museums; Public Relations; Natural History; Science and Technology (CIMUSET); Museum Security (ICMS); Glass. Affiliated International Associations include: Agricultural Museums (IAMA); Arms and Military History; Association of European Open-Air Museums; Performing Arts (SIBMAS); Transport Museums (IATM).

Membership is open to individuals and institutions. The support and services of ICOM are most required by museums in countries least able to afford them, and for this an independent tax-exempt foundation has been established to obtain and make available funds in support of ICOM, its members and their association, as well as other organizations with similar aims. ICOM holds a Triennial World Conference; meetings of National and International Committees; and special conferences and seminars.

REGIONAL AGENCIES: ICOM maintains the ICOM Regional Agency in Asia, in New Delhi, India; and encourages regional programs in cooperation with other related organizations in Africa, Latin America, and Arab countries.

PUBLICATIONS: *ICOM News,* quarterly; *International Museological Bibliography,* annual; Reports and Papers on Museums series, papers from symposiums and general conferences; *Museums' Annual: Education–Cultural Action,* annual, information on current events in museum education published by the ICOM International Committee for Education and Cultural Action since 1968; results of surveys, technical research, and committee recommendations; contributions to and cooperation in planning, distribution and sale of the UNESCO magazine, *Museum.*

UNESCO/ICOM DOCUMENTATION CENTRE: The Centre is an outgrowth of a library established in 1947 by the Museums and Monuments Division of UNESCO for its own research and documentation. The following year it was turned over to the International Council of Museums. It is administered by a small staff and maintains the largest library of its kind in existence. The responsibilities of the Centre are for: acquiring and conserving all documentation of any nature concerning subjects of interest to ICOM; making use of such information for purposes of diffusion and communicating the same to the personnel of UNESCO and to the members of ICOM, as well as, where possible, to all experts, students or qualified researchers; studying and using all means of improving and increasing the diffusion of information; encouraging the creation of regional documentation centers and coordinating their activities; assisting the National Committees and professional associations in the fields of documentation and information, more particularly by the instruction of trainees; assisting the International Committees in their documentary tasks (directories, questionnaires, cataloging), etc.; assisting the ICOM Secretariat in its tasks of a documentary, informative or bibliographical nature.

Documentation is received from all over the world and includes directories, manuals, treatises, monographs, guidebooks, and exhibition catalogues, photographs, architectural plans, bulletins and brochures. The material is analyzed, cross-referenced and classified in an extensive scheme based on the Library of Congress method. A card index system (Synoptic) permits the entire literature of a given museum subject to be consulted at the flip of a finger. The system can be readily adapted to a mechanical, microfilm or electronic system of documentation. Documents are then placed at the disposal of visitors at the Centre and correspondents. The Centre is able to furnish photocopies on request at cost price.

The Centre has established an international directory of museums, and index of suppliers; and is developing technical bibliographies. It publishes annually an international bibliography of basic museum writing covering publications appearing two years before.

AAM/ICOM: The United States National Committee merged with the American Association of Museums in 1973 to become AAM/ICOM. It is headquartered at the Association, 1055 Thomas Jefferson Street, N.W., Washington, D.C. 20007. (For details, see AAM description.)

United Nations Educational, Scientific and Cultural Organization (UNESCO), Place de Fontenoy, 75700 Paris, France.

The development of UNESCO programs began in 1924 when the League of Nations established the International Institute for Intellectual Cooperation, with a section designated the International Office of Museums. IOM published the bulletin *Mouseion;* a two-volume work, "Museographie"; and a number of technical manuals. Many of its projects were subsequently carried on by its successor, UNESCO.

UNESCO is an independent agency of the United Nations and has over 130 member states which contribute to its program. Its member states meet biennially and review and vote upon its program and budget. The program concerned with the preservation and development of cultural property is administered by the Department of Cultural Heritage which in turn is divided into two units.

The Monuments and Sites Division is concerned with the preservation, presentation and development of sites and monuments. It helps to organize research in scientific and technical aspects of the preservation of cultural property and the development of sites and monuments. It publishes technical manuals and books. Under the major part of the Division's program, member states are aided in the conservation of their sites and monuments through the provision of experts, fellowships and equipment under UNESCO's Program of Participation or through extra budgetary means, such as the United National Development Program (UNDP). Some of the projects are also aided through loans made by the International Bank for Reconstruction and Development (The World Bank) and the Inter-American Development Bank. It also carries out international campaigns for public and private contributions for such outstanding monuments as Philae (United Arab Republic), Borobudur (Indonesia), Moenjodaro (Pakistan), and the city of Venice (Italy).

The Museums and Norms Division helps to organize research in scientific and technical aspects for the preservation of movable cultural property. It publishes a quarterly, and is preparing a three-volume encyclopaedic work "Treatise on Museology." It also assists member states in the development of museums and in the conservation of cultural property under UNESCO's Program of Participation and has several projects for the development of museums financed under UNDP.

CONVENTIONS AND RECOMMENDATIONS: The Museums and Norms Division is responsible for the drafting and administration of international conventions adopted by the General Conference of UNESCO. To date, they include conventions: for the protection of cultural property in the event of armed conflict (The Hague, 1954); on the means of prohibiting and preventing the illicit export, import and transfer of ownership of cultural property (1970); concerning protection of the world cultural and natural heritage (1972). It has also drafted and administered international recommendations on the following subjects: on international principles applicable to archeological excavations (1956); concerning the most effective means of rendering museums accessible to everyone (1960); concerning safeguarding the beauty and character of landscapes and sites (1962); on the means of prohibiting and preventing the ilicit export, import and transfer of ownership of cultural property (1964); concerning the preservation of cultural property endangered by public or private works (1968); concerning protection, at the national level, of the cultural and natural heritage (1972). Two additional draft recommendations will be submitted to the General Conference of UNESCO in 1976 for adoption: the exchanges of original objects and specimens between institutions in different countries; the preservation of historic quarters, towns and sites and their integration in a modern environment.

PUBLICATIONS: *Museum,* quarterly; Museums and Monuments series, 15 volumes to date; conventions; recommendations.

TRAINING CENTERS: UNESCO has organized and operates, with the aid of a budget received from the UNDP regional program, regional training centers for the conservation of cultural property in cooperation with local authorities in: Jos, Nigeria, courses in French and English on preservation and on preparation of exhibitions; Chrubusco, Mexico, courses on preservation of movable cultural property; Cuzco, Peru, courses on preservation problems in the highland region and on conservation of sites; Baghdad, Iraq, courses on movable cultural property; Delhi, India, courses on movable cultural property.

INTERNATIONAL COOPERATION: UNESCO works closely with the International Centre for the Study of the Preservation and the Restoration of Cultural Property in Rome; the International Council of Monuments and Sites; and the International Council of Museums. It provides subventions to both ICOM and ICOMOS and has budgets to aid the operation of the international documentation centers in the fields of monuments and museums. UNESCO/ICOMOS International Documentation Center, 75 rue du Temple, 75003 Paris, France; UNESCO/ICOM Documentation Center, 1 rue Miollis, 75732 Paris 15e, France (see description under ICOM, above).

2

Role of Interpretation

The word *interpretation* conjures up a great number of philosophies, ideas, definitions and opinions. The chapter on Role of Interpretation includes references which deal with such issues as the museum's responsibility to interpret, the value of interpretation in the total museum program, the "language" of interpretation, and the status of museum educators. Reading these references will help to clarify the meaning of interpretation and its importance in museum programs, school services, exhibits, and media programs.

There are also notes on sources for museum education research and descriptions of professional museum educators organizations and committees at the end of the chapter.

Adam, Thomas R. *The Civic Value of Museums.* 1937. Reprint. Ann Arbor, Mich.: University Microfilms, 1974. 114 pp.

Adam, Thomas R. *The Museum and Popular Culture.* 1939. Reprint. Ann Arbor, Mich.: University Microfilms, 1974. 177 pp.

Alderson, William T. "Answering the Challenge," *Museum News,* 53:3 (November 1974), pp. 9ff. ♦ Describes the challenge to history museums as helping the American people understand themselves and their shared experience.

Allan, D. "The Role of Museums in Education," *Museums Journal,* 52:10 (January 1953), pp. 249-253.

Barnes, Frank. "Viewpoint: Living History, Clio or Cliopatra," *History News,* 29:9 (September 1974), pp. 202-203. ♦ Casts a critical eye on some kinds of historic site interpretation.

Barzun, Jacques. "Museum Piece, 1967," *Museum News,* 46:8 (April 1968), pp. 17-21.

Bassett, Richard, ed. *The Open Eye in Learning—The Role of Art in General Education.* Cambridge, Mass.: The MIT Press, 1969. 216 pp., illus., bibliog.

Borcoman, J. W. "Public Education in the

Visual Arts," *Curator,* XII:1 (March 1969), pp. 39-44.

Boulding, K. E. "The Role of the Museum in the Propagation of Developed Images," *Technology and Culture,* VII:1 (Winter 1966), pp. 64-66.

Brawne, Michael. *The New Museum: Architecture and Display.* New York: Frederick A. Praeger, 1966. 208 pp., photos, drawings, diagrams, graphs, bibliog., index of architects. ♦ Presents broad overview of the relationship of architecture and display in museums selected from around the world.

Brown, Henry D. "Intrigue Before You Instruct," *Museum News,* 42:7 (March 1964), pp. 28-33.

Cameron, Duncan F. "The Creative Audience," *The Museologist,* 114 (March 1970), pp. 12-19.

Cameron, Duncan F. "The "Language" of Museum Interpretation," *Journal of World History,* XIV:1 (1972), pp. 48-57. ♦ Contends that the "language" of interpretation frequently stands in the way of real communication.

Cameron, Duncan F. "The Museum: A Temple or the Forum," *Curator,* XIV:1 (March 1971), pp. 11-24. ♦ See also *Journal of World History,* XIV:1 (1972), pp. 189-202.

Cameron, Duncan F. "A Viewpoint: The Museum as a Communications System and Implications for Museum Education," *Curator,* XI:1 (March 1968), pp. 33-40. ◆ Defines those communication processes for which exhibits may be the medium of choice and concludes that education in museums should concentrate on the acquisition of visual learning skills in a manner akin to learning a language.

Cartwright, William H., and Richard L. Watson, eds. *The Reinterpretation of American History and Culture.* Washington, D.C.: National Council for the Social Studies, 1973. 554 pp., bibliog. ◆ Offers much bibliographical information and comments on important books which have appeared in the historical field.

Clay, George R. "Do Museums Educate?" *Museum News,* 39:2 (October 1960), pp. 36-40.

Coleman, Laurence Vail. *Manual for Small Museums.* New York: G. P. Putnam's Sons, 1927. 395 pp., illus., references.

Coleman, Laurence Vail. *The Museum in America: A Critical Study.* Washington, D.C.: American Association of Museums, 1939. 3 vols. ◆ This has been republished, with some parts of Vol. III omitted, by Museum Publications, Washington, D.C.

Daifuku, Hiroshi. "The Museum and the Visitor." In *The Organization of Museums: Practical Advice* (Paris: UNESCO, 1960), pp. 73-80. ◆ Discusses the reaction of visitors to exhibits, attempts to attract a wider public, and facilities to encourage visitors.

Dale, C. Kenny. "Fundamentals of Interpretive Planning," *Guideline,* 13:1 (September 1969), 3 pp.

Dale, Edgar. *Can You Give the Public What It Wants? The Need for Better Communication in Editing, Writing, Broadcasting, Advertising, Public Relations and Teaching.* New York: World Book Encyclopedia, 1967. 220 pp.

Dobbs, Stephen Mark. "Dana and Kent and Early Museum Education," *Museum News,* 50:2 (October 1971), pp. 38-41. ◆ Discusses two men influential in the history of museum education.

Education in the Art Museum. Proceedings of a Conference of Art Museum Educators held in Cleveland, Ohio, November 1971. New York: Association of Art Museum Directors, 1971. 85 pp., bibliog. ◆ Makes recommendations on the role of the museum education department in the operations and priorities of the art museum.

Ellsworth, Lucius F., and Maureen O'Brien, eds. *Material Culture: Historical Agencies and the Historian.* Philadelphia: Bode Reprint Service, 1969. 336 pp. ◆ Discusses how artifacts can be studied to expand understanding of the people who made them artifacts. Part I: *Material Culture: Theory, Method and Applications.* Part II: *Historical Agencies: Definition and History.*

ERIC Clearinghouse on Media and Technology. *Museums and Media: A Status Report,* prepared by Richard Grove; and *Museums and Media: A Basic Reference Shelf,* by Philip C. Ritterbush. Stanford, Calif.: ERIC Clearinghouse on Educational Media and Technology at the Institute for Communication Research, Stanford University, 1970. 15 pp. ◆ Based on a paper prepared for the President's Commission on Instructional Technology in 1968. Bibliography lists books, papers, periodicals and reports to help show the important role museums play in elementary and secondary education.

Exploration of the Ways, Means and Values of Museum Communication with the Viewing Public. New York: Museum of the City of New York, 1969. 80 pp., illus.

Fischer, David W. "The Role of Interpretation," *Guideline,* 20:1 (May 1966), 4 pp. ◆ Analyzes the crucial role interpretation plays in park management and introduces a new concept, "three M's" (material, media and market), to interpretive programs.

Fox, Thurman O. *Educational Programs.* AASLH Cassette Tape no. 5. Nashville, Tenn.: American Association for State and Local History, 1972. 56 minutes. ◆ A comprehensive survey of possible educational activities for the historical society including uses by scholars and children, orientation programs, movie programs, lecture series, institutes, developing school history programs with teachers, area research centers, educational kits, historymobiles.

Friedberg, Bernard. "Museums Collaborative: A Broker for Cooperation," *Museum News,* 52:7 (April 1974), pp. 20-24. ◆ Describes Museums Collaborative, an agency whose two major goals are to assist museums in decentralization of their resources and to provide joint services to museum education departments.

Frye, L. Thomas. "The Recent Past is Prologue," *Museum News,* 53:3 (November 1974), pp. 24-27. ◆ Discusses why history museums should concern themselves with events from the recent past and present. Outlines some creative approaches undertaken by museums, libraries, and related groups in collecting and interpreting recent history.

Funke, Mary Louise. "Mass Education and the Visual Arts," *Curator,* XII:1 (March 1969), pp. 60-70.

Gilborn, Craig A. "Pop Pedagogy," *Museum News,* 47:4 (December 1968), pp. 12-18. ◆ A study of the Coca-Cola bottle to typify the meaning of an object.

Gilborn, Craig. "Words and Machines: The Denial of Experience," *Museum News,* 47:1 (September 1968), pp. 25-29.

Godwin, Mabel W. "Museum Educational Facilities," *Museum,* VI:4 (1953), pp. 224-227.

Grove, Richard. "Some Problems in Museum Education." In *Museums and Education* (Washington, D.C.: Smithsonian Institution Press, 1968), pp. 79-85.

Guthe, Carl E. *The Management of Small History Museums.* 2nd ed. Nashville, Tenn.: American Association for State and Local History, 1969. 78 pp., bibliog. ◆ Chapter on Interpretation covers study and investigation, exhibits and supplementary services. Sound advice for both professional and volunteer.

Guthe, Carl E. *So You Want a Good Museum: A Guide to the Management of Small Museums.* 1957. Reprint. Washington, D.C.: American Association of Museums, 1967. 37 pp.

Hale, John. "Museums and the Teaching of History," *Museum,* XXI:1 (1968), pp. 67-72. ◆ Describes means of relating objects to complex historical situations in order to increase historical awareness.

Harrison, Molly. *Changing Museums: Their Use and Misuse.* London: Longmans, Green, and Co., Ltd., 1967. 110 pp., illus., bibliog.

Harvey, Dennis, and Bernard Friedberg, eds. *A Museum for the People: A Report of Proceedings at the Seminar on Neigborhood Museums held November 20, 21, and 22, 1969 at MUSE, the Bedford Lincoln Neighborhood Museum in Brooklyn, New York.* New York: Arno Press, 1971. 86 pp., illus.

Heslin, James J. "Does the Museum of History Teach History?" In *Museums and Education* (Washington, D.C.: Smithsonian Institution Press, 1968), pp. 153-165.

Hofmann, Helmut, and Leonard G. Johnson. "Translating Inert to Living Knowledge," *Curator,* V:2 (1962), pp. 120-127.

Hughes, Robert. "The Museum on Trial," *New York Times Magazine,* September 9, 1973, pp. 34ff. ◆ Suggests that museums are trying to be too "relevant"—competing with television and movies for a share of public attention.

Jelinek, Jan. "The Fields of Knowledge and Museums," *Journal of World History,* XIV:1 (1972), pp. 13-23. ◆ Presents several views and ideas on the phase and the role of modern museums in the world of knowledge.

Kennedy, Michael. "An Empirical Imperative: Education Must Become Museum Lexicon," *Museum News,* 46:6 (February 1968), pp. 31-33. ◆ Discusses the need to make explicit the essential educational function of museums.

Kepes, Gyorgy, ed. *The Visual Arts Today.* Middletown, Conn.: Wesleyan University Press, 1960. 272 pp., illus.

Kinard, John. "To Meet the Needs of Today's Audience," *Museum News,* 50:9 (May 1972), pp. 15-19.

Krepela, Rick. "To Tell the Story . . . Interpretation on a Nationwide Scale," *Museum News,* 48:7 (March 1970), pp. 42-45.

Low, Theodore. *The Museum as a Social Instrument.* New York: Metropolitan Museum of Art for the American Association of Museums, 1942. 70 pp., bibliog. ◆ Out-of-print. Describes institutional changes needed to establish educational capacity in museums. His arguments against prevailing conventions in school tours and exhibit technique may still be read with profit.

Low, Theodore. "The Museum as a Social Instrument: Twenty Years After," *Museum News,* 40:5 (January 1962), pp. 28-30.

Lynes, Russell. *The Tastemakers.* 1954. Reprint. New York: Grosset & Dunlap (by arrangement with Harper and Bros.), 1972. 362 pp., illus., bibliog.

McCabe, G. I., comp. *Education Through Museums: A Bibliography.* London: Group for Educational Services in Museums, 1972. 8 pp., ◆ Most of the references are to British publications.

McLuhan, Marshall. *Understanding Media: The Extensions of Man.* 2nd ed. New York: New American Library, 1973. 364 pp.

"McLuhanism in the Museum," *Museum News,* 46:7 (March 1968), pp. 11-18.

Matthai, Robert A. "In Quest of Professional Status," *Museum News,* 52:7 (April 1974), pp. 10-13. ◆ Argues that museum educators must define themselves more as educators than as inferior curators and should make their practices more professional.

Moe, Henry Allen. "The Role and Obligations of Museums as a Scholarly Resource." In *Museums and Education* (Washington, D.C.: Smithsonian Institution Press, 1968), pp. 25-34.

Munro, Thomas. *Art Education, Its Philosophy and Psychology: Selected Essays.* New York: Bobbs-Merrill Co., 1956. 387 pp. ◆ Includes articles on the function of the museum as an educational instrument, its methods and aims.

Murphey, John T. "What You Can Do With Your Education Department," *Museum News,* 49:2 (October 1970), pp. 14-17.

Museums Association. *Useful Addresses for Museum Curators.* Museums Association Information Sheet no. 2. London: The Association, 1972. 8 pp., paperback. ◆ List of addresses to help museum curators locate the manufacturers and suppliers (British) of specialized equipment and materials required by museums.

Naumer, Helmuth. "A Marketable Product," *Museum News,* 50:2 (October 1971), pp. 14-16. ◆ Argues that museums should revamp some of their traditional attitudes and become more cognizant of their educational tasks.

Naumer, Helmuth J. *Museum Education Programs.* AASLH Cassette Tape no. 18. Nashville, Tenn.: American Association for State and Local History, 1972. 51 minutes. ◆ Using experimental programs at the Fort

Worth Museum of Science and History as illustrations, shortcomings in the museum educational system are described. Discusses problems of museum education and some of the needs museum education must fill.

Nyquist, Ewald B. "Museums as an Educational Resource: the Position of the Regents," *The Museologist,* 10 (December 1966), pp. 13-21. ◆ Describes the relationship of the University of the State of New York to New York State museums.

Parker, Arthur C. *A Manual for History Museums.* New York; AMS Press, 1935. 204 pp., illus., bibliog. ◆ A standard comprehensive work which covers building, funding, exhibits, collections, research, school programs and publications.

Parker, Harley W. "The Museum as a Communication System," *Curator,* VI:4 (1963), pp. 350-360.

Parr, Albert E. "Temporary Exhibition Versus Education," *Curator,* V:4 (1962), pp. 369-370.

Pitman, Bonnie L., ed. *Southeast Museums Conference Directory of Education Programs and Resources.* New Orleans: Southeast Museums Conference of the American Association of Museums, 1974. 162 pp., bibliog. ◆ Includes program descriptions of eighty-six institutions in the twelve state southeast region as well as education staff listings; a compendium of resource people and organizations with expertise in such areas as administration, community development, docent training and exhibitions; bibliography of publications in education, exhibits, media, etc., used by professionals. Available from Bonnie Pitman, Curator of Education, New Orleans Museum of Art, P.O. Box 19123, New Orleans, Louisiana 70179.

Rath, Frederick, L., Jr. *The Cost of Freedom.* President's Address at the Twenty-second Annual Meeting of the American Association for State and Local History. Madison, Wisc.: American Association for State and Local History, 1962. 13 pp.

Read, Herbert. *Education Through Art.* London: Faber and Faber, 1943. 320 pp., illus., diagrams, bibliog. ◆ Also available from Transatlantic Arts, North Village Green, Levittown, Long Island, New York 11756.

Richardson, Edgar P. "The Museum and Education." In *Museums and Education*

(Washington, D.C.: Smithsonian Institution Press, 1968), pp. 11-23.

Ripley, S. Dillon. "Museums and Education," *Curator,* XI:3 (September 1968), pp. 183-189. ♦ Describes three distinct levels on which museum work and museum education should coincide, from the needs of the uninitiated to those of the advanced scholar.

Ripley, S. Dillon. *The Sacred Grove: Essays on Museums.* New York: Simon and Schuster, 1969. 159 pp., bibliog. references. ♦ A deft interweaving of educational and cultural elements in museum progra s.

Robbins, Michael W. "The Neighborhood and the Museum," *Curator,* XIV:1 (March 1971), pp. 63-68.

Ronsheim, Robert D. "Is the Past Dead?" *Museum News,* 53:3 (November 1974), pp. 16-18, 62. ♦ Points up some common pitfalls in interpretation and calls for careful thought and planning and the exercise of proper control in achieving a worthwhile program.

Ross, Beverly John. *Museum Resources and Their Utilization in Industrial Arts Education.* Doctoral Dissertation in Education at New York University, 1971. 358 pp. ♦ Available in microfilm from University Microfilms, Ann Arbor, Michigan.

Ruesch, Jurgen, and Weldon Kees. *Nonverbal Communication: Notes on the Visual Perception of Human Relations.* Berkeley: University of California Press, 1969. 205 pp., illus., bibliog.

Scanlon, Carole T. "Interpretation: The Language of the Visitor," *Historic Preservation,* 26:4 (October-December 1974), pp. 34-37.

Schoener, Allon. "The Electronic Museum," *Popular Photography,* April 1967. ♦ Reprinted in *The Museologist,* 116 (September 1970), pp. 17-25. Suggests that museums of the future will have to act as electronic communication centers from which verbal and visual information will be transmitted by a variety of communication media—telephones, videophones, radio, television, computers.

Screven, C. G. "The Museum as a Responsive Learning Environment," *Museum News,* 47:10 (June 1969), pp. 7-10. ♦ Explores some psychological aspects of museums, obstacles in their communication processes and pos-

sibilities for improvement derived from research in learning.

Shedd, Charles E., Jr. "Relevant Interpretation," *Midwest Region Interpretive Newsletter,* August, 1961. 3 pp. ♦ Deals with adapting interpretation to a changing audience.

Smithsonian Institution Conference on Museums and Education, University of Vermont, 1966. *Museums and Education: Papers.* Edited by Eric Larrabee. Washington, D.C.: Smithsonian Institution Press, 1968. 255 pp., bibliog. ♦ Contains some thought-provoking essays on museum education, its current status, its techniques, its function in various kinds of museums and its prospects for the future.

Stowell, Alice M. *The Living Museum.* 1st ed. New York: Vantage Press, 1956. 88 pp.

Taylor, Walter W. "Museums and Education," *Museum,* XXIII:2 (1970-1971), pp. 125-128.

Thomas, W. Stephen. "Museums and the Education Explosion," *The Museologist,* 114 (March 1970), pp. 5-11.

Thurman, Sue. "Museums and Education: The Role of the Art Object." In *Museums and Education.* (Washington, D.C.: Smithsonian Institution Press, 1968), pp. 139-152.

Tilden, Freeman, *Interpreting Our Heritage.* Rev. ed. Chapel Hill, N.C.: University of North Carolina Press, 1967. 120 pp., illus. ♦ Develops a philosophy of interpretation which points up the need to involve visitors in the interpretation and to make sites meaningful for them.

Tjerandsen, Carl. "The Museum in Adult Education," *Museum News,* 41:2 (October 1962), pp. 27-31. ♦ Argues that the museum has an obligation to make an educational contribution to society.

United Nations Educational, Scientific and Cultural Organization. *Museum Techniques in Fundamental Education.* Paris: UNESCO, 1957. 54 pp., illus., bibliog.

United Nations Educational, Scientific, and Cultural Organization. *Museums, Imagination and Education.* Paris: UNESCO, 1973. 148 pp., illus.

United Nations Educational, Scientific and Cultural Organization. *The Organization of Museums; Practical Advice.* Museums and

Monuments IX. Paris: UNESCO, 1960. 188 pp., 44 pp. photos, appendix, bibliog.

United Nations Educational, Scientific and Cultural Organization. *Recommendation Concerning the Most Effective Means of Rendering Museums Accessible to Everyone.* Adopted by the General Conference at its 11th session, Paris, December 14, 1960. Paris: UNESCO, 1960. 11 pp.

United Nations Educational, Scientific and Cultural Organization. Education Clearing House. *Some Papers on the Role of Museums in Education.* Paris: UNESCO, 1952. 37 pp., bibliog.

Warner, Charles W. "The Interpretation of an Historic Area through the Original Environment and the Visitor Center," *Guideline,* 16:1 (November 1963), 3 pp.

Washburn, Wilcomb E. "The Museum's Responsibility in Adult Education," *Curator,* VII:1 (1964), pp. 33-38.

White, Anne. *Visiting Museums.* New York: International Publications Service, 1968. 124 pp., illus.

Whitehill, Walter Muir. "The Bed of Procrustes," *The Museologist,* 129 (December 1973), pp. 6-16. ♦ Discusses trend of museums to try to be "relevant" when this is not their role.

Wittlin, Alma S. *The Museum: Its History and Its Tasks in Education.* London: Routledge and Kegan Paul, Ltd., 1949. 297 pp., illus., bibliog. references. ♦ Long the best known and still the standard work on museums and their educational role.

Wittlin, Alma S. *Museums: In Search of a Usable Future.* Cambridge, Mass.: MIT Press, 1970. 299 pp., illus., bibliog. references.

NOTES AND PERIODICALS

American Association of Museums, President's Education Committee. This committee was formed to improve communication primarily among museum educators and secondarily among all museum professionals.

Council on Museums and Education in the Visual Arts. This Council was formed in 1973 "to oversee an examination of visual arts education in museums." Its aims are to assemble a series of case studies, in a variety of educational areas in which art museums are operating and to focus on those programs and those aspects of them that can be instructive to others; to help museum educators enlarge the range and, if possible, raise the level of their discourse with each other and to promote rational inquiry into the basic purpose of museum education; and, to help develop networks of communication between museum educators and the world of education at large.

The information gathered for this project is to be published as a printed report for the museum profession, for schools, government agencies, educators and anyone interested in the educational role of museums.

ERIC Clearinghouse on Media Technology, Stanford University, Stanford, California 94305. The ERIC Clearinghouse is a national information system to provide ready access to the results of exemplary programs, research and development efforts and related information in the fields of education. ERIC = Educational Resources Information Center.

George Washington University, School of Education, Washington, D.C. 20006. George Washington University, School of Education is offering a Master of Arts program in Teaching–Museum Education. It provides preparation for education work in museums or liaison positions between museums and school systems. It includes course work in museum studies and an area of specialization such as anthropology, American civilization, fine arts or zoology, field work in elementary and secondary schools and an internship in the education department of a museum or similar institution.

Group for Educational Services in Museums. GESM is a professional organization of those whose full-time job is the promotion and development of museum education. Activities include conferences and courses. Publications include: *Newsletter,* three times per year; *Museum School Services,* a comprehensive guide to museum education services in the United Kingdom; *Museum Education Services,* addresses and facilities of services throughout the country. Chairman: Frank Hawtin, Weir Lodge, Staplegrove Road, Taunton, Somerset, England.

Guideline. 1971, bimonthly, subscription. National Conference on State Parks, Park Practice Program, 1601 North Kent Street, Arlington, Virginia 22209. ◆ Program members exchange methods of management, administration and interpretation of park and recreation facilities.

Midwest Region Interpretive Newsletter. 1973, quarterly. National Park Service, Midwest Regional Office, 1709 Jackson Street, Omaha, Nebraska 68102. ◆ Distributed as a means of communicating to the field information regarding the interpretive and curatorial activities and methodology of interest to Park Service museums in the Region.

Museum Education Forum, c/o Linda Sweet, Brooklyn Museum, 188 Eastern Parkway, Brooklyn, New York 11238. The Forum was organized by Museums Collaborative. It is concerned with the content and evaluation of museum education programs for school and non-school audiences; the training of museum educators; the role of museum educators within the museum structure. Activities include a program of meetings and workshops and a directory for New York City museum educators on current programs. Membership is informal with no dues.

Museum Education Roundtable, 1227 G Street, N.W., Washington, D.C. 20005. The Roundtable is a nonprofit organization dedicated to an exchange of information and ideas which will lead to improved education services in museums and other public institutions in the Washington metropolitan area. It is concerned with museum–school cooperation, in–service training for museum educators, docent training and evaluation. Activities: meetings, workshops and other events relevant to various aspects of museum education. Publications: *The Directory,* a guide to museums, parks, historic sites, and nature centers in the Washington area; *Roundtable Reports,* a quarterly newsletter of information and commentary about museum education trends in Washington and around the country.

Museums Collaborative, 830 Fifth Avenue, New York, New York 10021. Museums Collaborative has two goals: to assist museums in decentralizing their resources and in using these resources in novel ways to reach new audiences; to provide joint services to museum education departments including fund raising, publicity and information exchange. It is affiliated with the New York City Department of Cultural Affairs.

Trends. 1968, quarterly, subscription. National Conference on State Parks, Park Practice Program, 1601 North Kent Street, Arlington, Virginia 22209. ◆ A selection of readings on new and important issues relating to parks, recreation and conservation.

3
Visitor Surveys

Museum programs are not conducted, nor are exhibits designed, for the benefit of the museum staff. They are, rather, intended for the enjoyment and enlightenment of the visitor. Therefore it is important to know who that visitor is, what he brings to the museum and how he responds to the programs offered. In order to obtain that kind of information, a number of surveys and visitor analyses have been conducted. The references in the chapter on visitor surveys describe these studies, both in terms of methods used and results obtained. Taken as a whole, this chapter can provide the reader with an overview of the research which has been done in this area.

Abbey, D. S., and Duncan Cameron. "Investigating a Museum's Audience," *The Museologist,* 77 (December 1960), pp. 2-7.

Abbey, D. S., and Duncan Cameron. "Museum Audience Research," *Museum News,* 40:2 (October 1961), pp. 34-38.

Abbey, D. S., and Duncan Cameron. "Museum Audience Research: The Effect of an Admission Fee," *Museum News,* 41:3 (November 1962), pp. 25-28.

Abbey, David S., and Duncan F. Cameron. *The Museum Visitor: I—Survey Design.* Reports from Information Services, 1. Toronto: Royal Ontario Museum, 1959. 12 pp., illus., bibliog. ◆ Review of procedures followed in setting up a visitor survey.

Abbey, David S., and Duncan F. Cameron. *The Museum Visitor: III—Supplementary Studies.* Reports from Information Services, 3. Toronto: Royal Ontario Museum, 1961. 16 pp., graphs, charts, tables. ◆ Follow-up studies on the Royal Ontario Museum visitor survey.

Abbey, D. S., and Duncan Cameron. "Notes on Audience Research at the Royal Ontario Museum," *The Museologist,* 80 (September 1961), pp. 11-16. ◆ Pilot study on public reaction to admission charge for a public museum.

American Association of Museums. *Museums: Their New Audience.* A Report to the Department of Housing and Urban Development by a special committee of the American Association of Museums. Washington, D.C.: American Association of Museums, 1972. 108 pp., illus., diagrams, bibliog.

Bechtel, Robert B. "Hodometer Research in Museums," *Museum News,* 45:7 (March 1967), pp. 23-26.

Bechtel, Robert B. "Human Movement & Architecture," *Trans–Action,* 4:6 (May 1967), pp. 53-56. ◆ The hodometer, a floor grid sensitive to pedestrian movement, is fitted to a small room or gallery and apparatus to count movement is stationed in a nearby room. Bechtel monitors changes in locometer exploratory behavior as a function of environmental cues such as different displays or paintings.

Bigman, S. K. "Art Exhibit Audiences: Selected Findings on Who Comes? Why? With What Effects?" *The Museologist,* 59 (June 1956), pp. 6-16; 60 (September 1956), pp. 2-6.

Borhegyi, Stephan F. de. "Testing of Audience Reaction to Museum Exhibits," *Curator,* VIII:1 (1965), pp. 86-93.

Borhegyi, Stephan F. de, and Irene A. Hanson. "Chronological Bibliography of Museum Visitor Surveys." In *Museums and Education* (Washington, D.C.: Smithsonian Institution Press, 1968), pp. 239-251.

Borhegyi, Stephan F. de, and Irene A. Hanson, eds. *The Museum Visitor: Selected Essays and Surveys of Visitor Reaction to Exhibits in the Milwaukee Public Museum . . . .* Milwaukee, Wisc.: Milwaukee Public Museum, 1968. 187 pp., charts, tables.

Cameron, Duncan F. "How Do We Know What Our Visitors Think?" *Museum News,* 45:7 (March 1967), pp. 31-33. ◆ Advice about studies of visitors which may be concluded even by small museums, and criticisms of careless data gathering programs not readily translatable into improvements in visitor services.

Cameron, Duncan F., and David S. Abbey. *The Museum Visitor: II-Survey Results.* Reports from Information Services, 2. Toronto: Royal Ontario Museum, 1960. 38 pp., illus., tables, appendices. ◆ Report on a typical visitor survey, emphasizing demographic and descriptive variables.

Cameron, Duncan F., and David S. Abbey. "Visits Versus Visitors: An Analysis," *Museum News,* 39:3 (November 1960), pp. 34-35. ◆ Describes a survey of visitor population versus total attendance conducted at the Royal Ontario Museum.

Campbell, Donald T., and Julian C. Stanley. *Experimental and Quasi-Experimental Designs for Research.* Chicago: Rand McNally and Co., 1966. 84 pp., illus., bibliog. ◆ Classic discussion of experimental design.

Christensen, Erwin O. "Evening Hours for Museums: A Preliminary Statistical Survey," *Museum News,* 43:3 (November 1964), pp. 40-41.

Loomis, Ross J. "Museums and Psychology: The Principle of Allometry and Museum Visitor Research," *The Museologist,* 129 (December 1973), pp. 17-23.

Loomis, Ross J. "Please! Not Another Visitor Survey," *Museum News,* 52:2 (October 1973), pp. 21-26.

MacBriar, Wallace N., Jr. "Testing Your Audience," *Museum News,* 42:8 (April 1964), pp. 15-17.

Morris, Rudolph. "Leisure Time and the Museum," *Museum News,* 41:4 (December 1962), pp. 17-21.

New York (State) University, State Education Department, Division of Evaluation. *The 1966 Audience of the New York State Museum: An Evaluation of the Museum's Visitor Programs.* Albany: The University, 1968. 160 pp. ◆ Study includes geographic distribution, characteristics (sex, age, occupation, education, income level), and visitor behavior.

Parr, A. E. "Location, Motivation, and Duration of Museum Attendance," *Curator,* X:3 (September 1967), pp. 206-210.

Smits, Edward J. "A Suburban Museum Looks at its Visitors," *Museum News,* 42:9 (May 1964), pp. 30-34. ◆ Describes successful survey techniques used at the Nassau County (N.Y.) Historical Museum.

Washburne, Randel F., and J. Alan Wagar. "Evaluating Visitor Response to Exhibit Content," *Curator,* XV:3 (September 1972), pp. 248-254.

4

Museum Programs

Every museum, historic site, and historical society serves many different publics: the tourist, the local history buff, children, adults, the handicapped, the community as a whole and the special groups within it. And these historical organizations have an obligation to make every effort to serve these different groups. To do so, most organizations have developed a wide variety of programs. Exhibits and school services will be dealt with separately in succeeding chapters. The complex of other programs offered are covered in this chapter, Museum Programs.

The General Reference section includes surveys of existing and potential museum programs. In–Museum Programs includes a number of different activities which are conducted on the premises of the historical society or museum: orientation programs, training and use of docents, guides and volunteers, the special problems of historic site interpretation and living history programs, adult education and other programs.

Museum Extension Services includes those activities which are conducted outside the historical organization and frequently in conjunction with other cultural or community agencies. Guidebooks and Walking Tours offers a sampling (by no means a complete list) of publications designed to familiarize people with the historic and architectural heritage of their communities. Also included are a few references which provide guidelines for planning walking tours. Community Programs covers a wide range of activities: ethnic studies, environmental education, oral history, neighborhood museums, community festivals, historic marker programs. A special section provides references to programs generated by the Bicentennial. Again, this is not a comprehensive list but a selection of the kinds of activities and publications which resulted from the Bicentennial impetus. Travelling Museums includes references on mobile extensions of museums; travelling exhibits are covered in the chapter on exhibits. All of these extension programs are ways of moving the museum outside its own walls and expanding its public. They bring the museum and its resources to people who will not or cannot come to the museum themselves.

The last three sections of the chapter—Junior Programs, Children's Museums, and Museum Programs for the Handicapped—provide references on very specialized programs for these groups with particular needs.

General Reference

Anderson, Scarvia B. "Noseprints on the Glass or How Do We Evaluate Museum Programs." In *Museums and Education* (Washington, D.C.: Smithsonian Institution Press,

1968), pp. 115-126. ◆ Discusses the general problem of evaluating the educational merit of programs in atypical settings such as museums, field trips, etc.

Coleman, Laurence Vail. "Educational Work." In *Manual for Small Museums* (New

York: G. P. Putnam's Sons, 1927), pp. 241-290. ◆ Includes activities for children, school service, adult education, the museum library, publications, and publicity.

Golden, Hal, and Kitty Hanson. *How to Plan and Publicize Special Events.* Dobbs Ferry, N.Y.: Oceana Publications, 1960. 256 pp., illus.

Newsom, Barbara Y. *The Metropolitan Museum as an Educational Institution: A Study with Recommendations.* New York: The Metropolitan Museum, 1970. 126 pp., bibliog.

Rogers, Lola Erikson. *Museums and Related Institutions; A Basic Program Survey.* Washington, D.C.: U.S. Office of Education, 1969. 120 pp., illus., graphs, tables. ◆ Based upon a pioneering survey of 2889 establishments considered to conform to a working definition of museum, this study was undertaken for the U.S. Office of Education in cooperation with the Smithsonian Institution and the American Association of Museums. It provides important overall information on governing authority, type of exhibits, location by city and state, paid and volunteer staff, study facilities, level of operating expenditure, number of annual visits, and educational service.

Walton, Ann. "The Computerized Magical Mystery Tour," *Museum News,* 51:8 (April 1973), pp. 18-20. ◆ Describes how the Denver Art Museum computerized its tour requests and docent schedules.

Williams, R. D. "The Search for New Program Ideas," *History News,* 15:10 (August 1960), pp. 126-127.

Williamson, Moncrieff. "Communications and the Small Museum," *Museum News,* 46:3 (November 1967), pp. 13-17. ◆ Discusses extension services and the small museum.

In-Museum Programs

Orientation Programs

Alexander, Edward P. "An Orientation Program for Colonial Williamsburg," *Museum News,* 26:20 (April 15, 1949), pp. 7-8.

Appleman, Roy. E. "An Historical Interpretive Center," *Museum News,* 20:13 (January 1, 1943), pp. 10-12.

Dailey, Daniel, and Roger Mandle. "Welcome to the Museum," *Museum News,* 52:5 (January-February 1974), pp. 45-49.

Gaines, William. "Virginia Museum: Two Pioneer Programs," *Museum News,* 50:2 (October 1971), pp. 22-25.

Thomas, W. Stephen. "A New Museum Orientation Theatre: An Experiment in Interpreting Exhibits at the Rochester Museum and Science Center," *The Museologist,* 122 (March 1972), pp. 18-20.

Docents, Guides, and Volunteers

Bay, Ann. "Getting Decent Docents," *Museum News,* 52:7 (April 1974), pp. 25-29. ◆ Describes a variety of interpreter programs.

Black, Patricia F. "Today's Youth, Tomorrow's Heritage: Teenage Docents at Old Economy," *Historic Preservation,* 24:2 (April-June 1972), pp. 18-21.

Bradshaw, Mary Claire. "Volunteer Docent Programs: A Pragmatic Approach to Museum Interpretation," *History News,* 28:8 (August 1973), Technical Leaflet no. 65.

Hake, Metta. *Advanced Training Handbook for Tour Guides.* Sacramento, Calif.: California Department of Parks and Recreation, 1971. 38 pp. ◆ Concentrates on speech training for guides. Has some practical suggestions for improving speech and for holding the attention of visitors to historic sites. Includes voice exercises.

Low, Shirley. "Training Interpreters," *Guideline,* 30:1 (April 1969), 12 pp. ◆ Gives details of the training program developed at Colonial Williamsburg for hosts and hostesses in the Exhibition Buildings.

Montgomery, Florence M. "The Training of Guides," *History News,* 19:5 (March 1964), Technical Leaflet no. 18 (old series).

Morgan, William L. "A Survey of American Museum Docent Programs," *Museum News,* 46:10 (June 1968), pp. 28-30.

Platt, Doris. "The Youthful Outlook: Teenage Docent Program at Old Economy," *History News,* 27:8 (August 1972), p. 177.

Reed, Betty Jane. "Establishing a Community Resource Volunteer Program," *Museum News,* 50:9 (May 1972), pp. 20-24.

Reibel, Daniel B., and Patricia Black. *A Manual for Guides, Docents, Hostesses, and Volunteers of Old Economy.* Ambridge, Pa.: Old Economy, The Harmonie Associates, 1970. various pagings, mimeo.

Wriston, Barbara. "Volunteer Programs in Museums of the United States," *The Museologist,* 113 (December 1969), pp. 5-12.

Historic Site Interpretation and Living History Programs

Alderson, William T., and Shirley P. Low. *Interpretation of Historic Sites.* Nashville, Tenn.: American Association for State and Local History, 1976. 189 pp., illus., bibliog., appendices, index. ◆ Considers the practical problems of developing and conducting interpretive programs, from setting objectives through evaluation of the established program.

Alexander, Edward P. "Bringing History to Life: Philadelphia and Williamsburg," *Curator,* IV:1 (1961), pp. 58-68.

Attention to Details–Do's and Don'ts of Historic House Intrepretation. Nashville, Tenn.: American Association for State and Local History, 1973. 5 minute cassette tape, slide carousel, supplementary material. Rental or purchase. ◆ The audience is asked to participate in discovering what is incorrect in several instances of historic house interpretation.

Barnes, Frank. "Viewpoint: Living History, Clio or Cliopatra," *History News,* 29:9 (September 1974), pp. 202-203. ◆ Casts a critical eye on some kinds of historic site interpretation.

Beazley, Elizabeth. *The Countryside on View: A Handbook on Countryside Centres, Field Museums and Historic Buildings Open to the Public.* London: Constable and Company, Ltd., 1971. 207 pp., illus., plans, bibliog., index.

Benedict, Paul. "Historic Site Interpretation: The Student Field Trip," *History News,* 26:3 (March 1971), Technical Leaflet no. 19.

Black, Patricia F. *The Live-In at Old Economy. An Experiment in a Role Playing Educational Program in the Museum.* Ambridge, Pa.: The Harmonie Associates, Inc., 1972. 42 pp., illus.

Colwell, Wayne. "Windows on the Past," *Museum News,* 50:10 (June 1972), pp. 36-38.

◆ Thoughts on communicating history through historic re-creations.

Cook, Peter W. "The Craft of Demonstrations," *Museum News,* 53:3 (November 1974), pp.10-15, 63. ◆ Gives basic information on setting up a practical working plan for craft demonstrations and offers a word of warning against token presentation programs.

DeLozier, Loretta. "Yosemite Finds a Way," *Midwest Region Interpretative Newsletter,* 16:21-22 (October-November 1971), 8 pp. ◆ Deals with "people problems" at Yosemite by humanizing the park experience for the modern visitors and shows how interpretation is adapted to various ages and types of people.

Helms, Mary Rhodes. "Jamestown Came Alive for Virginia School Children," *Discovery,* VI:1 (Winter 1974), 2 pp. ◆ Shows how one brings history alive for young children by having them use objects and by problem-solving.

"Hermitage Museum Lets Down the Bars," *History News,* 25:6 (June 1970), pp. 118-119.

Interpreting Healy House–Role Playing. Nashville, Tenn.: American Association for State and Local History, 1973. 5 minute cassette tape, slide carousel, supplementary material. Rental or purchase. ◆ Describes how guides at Healy House in Leadville, Colorado interpret history by living it.

Lewis, Steve. "Living History: An Active Interpretation of the Past," *Trends,* (October-November-December 1974), pp. 21-23.

Low, Shirley P. "Historic Site Interpretation: The Human Approach," *History News,* 20:11 (November 1965), Technical Leaflet no. 32.

Mahaffey, Ben D. *Relative Effectiveness and Visitor Preference of Three Audio-Visual Media for Interpretation of an Historic Area.* Departmental Information Report no. 1. College Station, Texas: Texas A&M University, 1969. 63 pp., illus., graphs, tables, forms, appendices, bibliog.

Schlebecker, John T. *Living Historical Farms: A Walk into the Past.* Washington, D.C. Smithsonian Institution Press, 1968. 31 pp., illus.

Schlebecker, John T. *The Past in Action: Living Historical Farms.* Washington, D.C.: Smithsonian Institution, 1967. 57 pp., bibliog., appendices.

Schlebecker, John T., and Gale E. Peterson. *Living Historical Farms Handbook.* Washington, D.C.: Smithsonian Institution Press, 1972. 91 pp., directories, index, bibliog. references. ◆ Contains specific organizational suggestions and a ten page listing of people throughout the country who are particularly interested in historical farms.

Shedd, Jeanne. "Education in Living History: An Historical Museum Experiment," *The Museologist,* 98 (March 1966), pp. 7-13. ◆ Describes an in-museum education program developed by a small historical society.

Sidford, Holly. "Stepping into History," *Museum News,* 53:3 (November 1974), pp. 28-35. ◆ Contends that in order for museums to use visitor participation programs effectively, visitors need a basic introduction to the museum's resources.

Tilden, Freeman. *Interpreting Our Heritage.* Rev. ed. Chapel Hill, N.C.: University of North Carolina Press, 1967. 120 pp., illus. ◆ Develops a philosophy of interpretation which points up the need to involve visitors in the interpretation and to make sites meaningful for them.

NOTES AND PERIODICALS

Association for Living Historical Farms and Agricultural Museums, Smithsonian Institution, Washington, D.C. 20560. The Association is interested in preserving historical farms and various aspects of agricultural history.

Living Historical Farms Bulletin. 1970, quarterly, membership. Association for Living Historical Farms and Agricultural Museums, Smithsonian Institution, Washington, D.C. 20560.

Adult Education

Gebhard, Bruno. "The Workshop Technique in Museum Education," *Museum News,* 29:11 (December 1, 1951), pp. 5-6.

Hunter, C. Bruce. "Museum Courses as a Service to the Community," *Curator,* I:2 (Spring 1958), pp. 53-56.

Miller, Harry L. *Teaching and Learning in Adult Education.* New York: MacMillan & Co., 1964. 340 pp., diagrams, bibliog. references.

Patterson, Joseph Allen. "Museum Programs in Education." In *Museums and Education* (Washington, D.C.: Smithsonian Institution Press, 1968), pp. 37-47.

Powell, Mary. "Library Methods that Museums Might Employ in the Field of Adult Education," *Museum News,* 28:18 (March 15, 1951), pp. 4-5.

Richman, Irwin. "A Guide to Planning Local History Institutes," *History News,* 22:8 (August 1967), Technical Leaflet no. 43.

Thomas, W. Stephen. "Museums and the Education Explosion," *The Museologist,* 114 (March 1970), pp. 5-11.

Tjerandsen, Carl. "The Museum in Adult Education," *Museum News,* 41:2 (October 1962), pp. 27-31. ◆ Argues that the museum has an obligation to make an educational contribution to society.

Washburn, Wilcomb, E. "The Museum's Responsibility in Adult Education," *Curator,* VII:1 (1964), pp. 33-38.

Zetterberg, Hans L. *Museums and Adult Education.* New York: A. M. Kelley for the International Council of Museums, 1969. 89 pp., illus., bibliog. ◆ A comprehensive discussion of the role of museums in adult education. Sponsored by the ICOM Committee for Education and Cultural Action with the assistance of UNESCO.

Other Programs

"Music Section: Music Programs at Museums," *Museum News,* 45:5 (January 1967), pp. 29-41.

Schmidt, Patricia C., et al. "Oral History," *History News,* May 1973-June 1976. ◆ A bimonthly column on oral history programs.

Smith, Arthur L. "Producing the Slide Show for Your Historical Society," *History News,* 22:6 (June 1967), Technical Leaflet no. 42.

"Vermont Group Utilizes Yankee Ingenuity," *History News,* 27:9 (September 1972), pp. 190-191. ◆ Describes programs at the McCullough Mansion, North Bennington, Vermont.

Museum Extension Services

Guidebooks and Walking Tours

Citizen's Association of Georgetown. *A Walking Guide to Historic Georgetown.* Washington, D.C.: Foundation for the Preservation of Historic Georgetown, 1971. 52 pp., illus., maps, bibliog.

Faison, Samson Lane. *Art Tours and Detours in New York State; A Handbook to More than Seventy-five Outstanding Museums and Historic Landmarks in the Empire State.* New York: Random House, 1964. 303 pp., illus., maps.

Holbert, Sue E., and June D. Holmquist. *A History Tour of 50 Twin City Landmarks.* St. Paul, Minn.: Minnesota Historical Society, 1966. 64 pp., illus., prints, maps, bibliog., index.

Huxtable, Ada Louise. *Four Walking Tours of Modern Architecture in New York City.* New York: Museum of Modern Art, 1961. 76 pp., illus.

Lestz, Gerald S. *Historic Heart of Lancaster: A Do-It-Yourself Guide for a Walking Tour of the Central Section of Lancaster, Pennsylvania, America's Oldest Inland City and County Seat of the Garden Spot of the World.* Lancaster, Pa.: J. Baer's Songs, 1962. 56 pp., illus., bibliog.

New York (State) University, State Education Department, Office of State History. *Sights and Sounds of New York State History.* Albany: The University, 1968. 52 pp.

Reed, Henry Hope. "A Primer on Walking Tours," *Museum News,* 53:3 (November 1974), pp. 20-23. ♦ Describes the walking tours conducted by the Museum of the City of New York. Delineates some general guidelines in setting up such a program.

Rettig, Robert B. *Guide to Cambridge Architecture: Ten Walking Tours.* Cambridge, Mass.: MIT Press, 1969. unpaged, illus., maps.

Van Trump, James D. *An Architectural Tour of Pittsburgh.* Rev. ed. The Stones of Pittsburgh no. 1. Pittsburgh: Pittsburgh History and Landmarks Foundation, 1968. 12 pp., illus.

Waite, Diana S. *A Walking Tour of Fifth Avenue, Troy, New York.* Troy, N.Y.: Fifth Avenue Association and Rensselaer County Historical Society, 1970. 18 pp., drawings, map.

Wheeler, Robert C. "Planning Tours for Your Historical Society," *History News,* 20:1 (January 1965), Technical Leaflet no. 25.

Community Programs

GENERAL PROGRAMS

Allison, David. "The Museum and the Immigrant," *Museums' Annual: Education—Cultural Action,* 2 (1970), pp. 25-27.

America the Beautiful Fund. *Old Glory: A Pictorial Report on the Grass Roots History Movement and the First Hometown History Primer.* New York: Warner Publishing Co., 1973. 191 pp., illus. ♦ Descriptions of America the Beautiful Fund projects.

American Association of Museums. Environmental Committee. *Museums and the Environment: A Handbook for Education.* New York: Arkville Press, 1971. 261 pp., illus., glossary, bibliog., appendices. ♦ A guide for museums, historical societies, schools and colleges interested in initiating exhibits and other educational projects dealing with human ecology. Gives instructions for developing themes around population, pollution, and environment.

"Anacostia," *History News,* 27:5 (May 1972), pp. 102-103.

Daley, Mary. "Heritages Preserved: Ethnic Crafts in Cleveland," *Historic Preservation,* 20:1 (January-March 1974), pp. 19-23. ♦ Describes Peoples and Cultures, Inc., a nonprofit organization, chartered in 1971 to celebrate the diverse ethnic heritage of Cleveland, Ohio.

The Foxfire Book: Hog Dressing, Log Cabin Building, Mountain Crafts and Foods; Planting by the Signs, Snake Lore, Hunting, Faith Healing, Moonshining, and Other Affairs of Plain Living. Edited by Eliot Wigginton. Garden City, N.Y.: Doubleday & Co., 1972. 384 pp., illus.

Foxfire Two: Ghost Stories, Spring Wild Plant Foods, Spinning and Weaving, Midwifing, Burial Customs, Cornshucking, Wagon Making and More Affairs of Plain Living. Garden City, N.Y.: Doubleday & Co. 1973. 410 pp., illus.

Frankforter, W. D. "The Community Festival as Practiced in Grand Rapids," *Museum News,* 48:5 (January 1970), pp. 20-23.

Henry, Delaura. "Heritages Preserved: Traditions in the Choctaw Homeland," *Historic Preservation,* 20:1 (January-March 1974), pp. 28-31. ♦ Describes aspects of Choctaw heritage and efforts to preserve it.

Idaho. Department of Highways. Public Information Section. *Idaho's Historical Sign Program.* Boise: Idaho Department of Highways, 1963. 32 pp., illus., fold. map.

McCalmon, George, and Christian Moe. *Creating Historical Drama: A Guide for the Community and the Interested Individual.* Carbondale, Ill.: Southern Illinois University Press, 1965. 393 pp., illus., bibliog.

National Education Association and National Park Service. *A Guide to Planning and Conducting Environmental Study Area Workshops.* Washington, D.C.: National Education Association, 1972. 50 pp., illus., bibliog. ♦ Gives detailed advice for planning, conducting and following through on environmental education workshops.

Wilcox, Arthur. "Historic Marking Along the Highways of America," *Planning and Civic Comment* (December 1961), pp. 23-32.

Willensky, Elliot. *Guide to Developing a Neighborhood Marker System.* New York: Museum of the City of New York, 1972. 63 pp., illus. ♦ Discusses how to identify the resources in the community and how to conduct the project.

Willensky, Elliot. *An Urban Information System for New York City.* New York: Museum of the City of New York, 1972. 203 pp., illus., appendices, bibliog.

THE BICENTENNIAL

American Revolution Bicentennial Administration. *Official Master Reference for Bicentennial Activities.* 2nd ed. Washington, D.C.: American Revolution Bicentennial Administration, 1974. 294 pp. ♦ To be revised and updated four times a year. Contains indexes and abstracts of Bicentennial Projects catalogued in the ARBA Bicentennial Information Network (BINET), a computerized information system. Printouts are available at a minimum charge of $15.00.

Cook, Anne H., and Jane T. Breinholt. *Project 1776: A Manual for the Bicentennial.* Rev. ed. Devon, Pa.: Pennsylvania Bicentennial Commission, 1974. 206 pp., illus., bibliog. ♦ Source book of history and learning ideas in Early American Culture for elementary school pupils.

Crouch, Tom D. *Ohio Bicentennial Guide: Suggestions for Commemorating the American Revolution Bicentennial.* Columbus, Ohio: Ohio Historical Society for the Ohio American Revolution Bicentennial Advisory Commission, 1973. 50 pp.

Hartje, Robert George. *Bicentennial USA; Pathways to Celebration.* Nashville, Tenn.: American Association for State and Local History, 1973. 334 pp., illus., bibliog. ♦ An approach to celebration based on a study of past centennials. Deals with the meaning and spirit of the Bicentennial for all Americans and provides a valuable list of activities that planners may adapt to the local situation.

Ireland, Willard E. "British Columbia Centennial: A Provincial Birthday Celebration," *History News,* 15:2 (December 1959), pp. 22-26.

Massachusetts Bicentennial Commission. *The Commemorative Guide to the Massachusetts Bicentennial.* Boston: Yankee, Inc., 1975. 160 pp., illus.

Massachusetts Bicentennial Commission. *Community Resources Handbook.* Boston: The Commission, 1974. 68 pp., bibliog. ♦ Contains ideas, references, contacts; a fully factual "how-to" booklet for local bicentennial planners.

National Trust for Historic Preservation. *Directory for Bicentennial Planning.* Washington, D.C.: The Trust, 1974. 62 pp. ♦ A source book for those seeking information or consultation on historic preservation for the Bicentennial. Lists individuals formally involved in planning Bicentennial preservation projects in the fifty states, U.S. territories and the District of Columbia.

National Trust for Historic Preservation. *Preservation for the Bicentennial.* Washington, D.C.: The Trust, 1971. ♦ An information packet on historic preservation that can be used as a tool for preliminary planning during the Bicentennial Era.

New York State American Revolution Bicentennial Commission. *A New York State Guide to Local Bicentennial Planning.* Albany: The Commission, 1974. 50 pp., bibliog.

People's Bicentennial Commission. *America's Birthday. A Planning and Activity Guide for Citizens' Participation During the Bicentennial Years.* New York: Simon & Schuster, 1974. 189 pp., illus.

NOTES AND PERIODICALS

American Revolution Bicentennial Administration, 2401 E Street, N.W., Washington, D.C. 20276. The main function of the ARBA is to provide leadership, motivation and coordination; to serve as a central clearinghouse and master calendar of events, projects, ceremonies and events of states, localities and private entities. It will coordinate federal and nonfederal programs, provide for project competitions and recognition of meritorious programs, and provide for preparation, distribution, dissemination and sale of exhibition, historical, commemorative and informative items.

Bicentennial Bulletin. 1971, weekly, free. American Revolution Bicentennial Administration, 2401 E Street, N.W., Washington, D.C. 20276. ◆ A newsletter of Bicentennial information.

Bicentennial Times. 1974, monthly, free. American Revolution Bicentennial Administration, 2401 E Street, N.W., Washington, D.C. 20276. ◆ *Bicentennial Times* replaced *Bicentennial Newsletter* (February 1972–September 1973) which replaced *Bicentennial Era* (February 1970–December 1971). Features information on Bicentennial activities and ARBA programs.

Common Sense. 1973, bimonthly, subscription. People's Bicentennial Commission, 1346 Connecticut Avenue, N.W., Room 1025, Washington, D.C. 20036.

People's Bicentennial Commission, 1346 Connecticut Avenue, N.W., Washington, D.C. 20036. The People's Bicentennial Commission was formed to return the Bicentennial celebration to the people. It develops ·Bicentennial programming, conducts workshops and provides speakers and materials for organizations.

Project 1776: A Bicentennial Program in Early American Culture for Elementary School Pupils. The purpose of Project 1776 is to enrich the social studies curriculum, specifically in colonial history, by recreating through sensory experiences the mood and life style that prevailed among the people at the time of our country's beginnings. It includes three phases: (1) in-service training for teachers, (2) demonstrations and related displays in schools using museum objects, (3) a field trip to an 18th century Pennsylvania farm where they live as children of 1776. It is supported by the Bicentennial Commission of Pennsylvania and the Commissioners of Chester County with the sponsorship of the Chester County Historical Society.

U.S.A. 200: The American Bicentennial Monthly. 1971, monthly, subscription. Bicentennial Council of the Thirteen Original States, c/o Brian Dow, Director of Public Information, Suite 2001, 400 Colony Square, Atlanta, Georgia 30361. ◆ Gives news and information on Bicentennial activities nationwide and particularly in the thirteen state area.

Travelling Museums

Grobman, Arnold. "Museum Extension Through Travelling Museums," *Curator,* I:4 (1958), pp. 82-88.

Hudson, David S. "The Artmobile: Fine Art on the Road," *Curator,* IX:4 (December 1966), pp. 337-355.

Munro, Alan R. "The Yellow Submarine," *Museum News,* 46:6 (February 1968), pp. 20-23. ◆ Describes mobile museum of the Children's Museum in Nashville, Tennessee.

Robbins, Michael. "SAM [Student Art Mobile] Explains," *Museum News,* 47:8 (April 1969), pp. 19-21.

"Rolling Museum Takes Education to Isolated Northern Canadians," *History News,* 29:1 (January 1974), pp. 6-7.

Supplee, Carol. "Museums on Wheels," *Museum News,* 53:2 (October 1974), pp. 26-35. ◆ Outlines some of the reasons why mobile programs are growing so rapidly and includes some practical information on operating such programs.

"Tactile Mobile Museum," *Environment Southwest,* 411 (April 1969), n.p.

Junior Programs

Bay, Ann. *Museum Programs for Young People.* Washington, D.C.: Smithsonian Institution, 1973. 282 pp., illus. ◆ Case studies of education programs in 14 American museums and discussion of programs of special interest. Includes information on exhibits, in-museum programs, extension services, staff, funding, coordination with schools, facilities and publications.

Benedict, Paul L. "Historic Site Interpretation: The Student Field Trip," *History News,* 26:3 (March 1971), Technical Leaflet no. 19.

Black, Patricia F. "Today's Youth, Tomorrow's Heritage: Teenage Docents at Old Economy," *Historic Preservation,* 24:2 (April-June 1972), pp. 18-21.

Coleman, Laurence Vail. "Educational Work." In *Manual for Small Museums* (New York: G. P. Putnam's Sons, 1927), pp. 241-290. ◆ Includes activities for children, school-service, adult education, the museum library, publications, and publicity.

The Foxfire Book: Hog Dressing, Log Cabin Building, Mountain Crafts and Foods; Planting by the Signs, Snake Lore, Hunting, Faith Healing, Moonshining, and Other Affairs of Plain Living. Edited by Eliot Wigginton. Garden City, N.Y.: Doubleday, 1972. 384 pp., illus.

Foxfire Two: Ghost Stories, Spring Wild Plant Foods, Spinning and Weaving, Midwifing, Burial Customs, Cornshucking, Wagon Making and More Affairs of Plain Living. Garden City, N.Y.: Doubleday, 1973. 410 pp., illus.

Gaines, William. "Virginia Museum: Two Pioneer Programs," *Museum News,* 50:2 (October 1971), pp. 22-25. ◆ Describes art mobiles and orientation theatres at the Virginia Museum of Fine Arts.

Gordon, Arthur. "The Magic Glow of Foxfire," *Reader's Digest* (November 1973), pp. 67-72. ◆ Condensed from the *Baltimore Sunday Sun,* August 26, 1973.

Harrison, Molly. *Museum Adventure: The Story of the Geoffrye Museum.* London: University of London Press, 1950. 176 pp., illus.

Hastie, Tom. *History After Four O'Clock; Some Suggestions for Those Concerned with School History Clubs.* London: Historical Association, 1971. 16 pp.

The History Club of Short High School. *Nineteenth Century Architecture: Liberty, Indiana.* Liberty, Ind.: History Club of Short High School, 1969. 16 pp., illus.

Indiana Junior Historical Society. *A Handbook for History Club Officers and Sponsors.* Indianapolis, Ind.: The Society, 1970. 25 pp., illus.

Indiana Junior Historical Society. *Our River: An Architectural and Historical Journey.* Indianapolis, Ind.: The Society, 1970. 38 pp., illus. ◆ A study of the architectural and historical elements along the Ohio River from Madison, Indiana to the mouth of the Wabash.

Indiana Junior Historical Society. *Oh, The Moonlight's Fair Tonight Along the Wabash.* Indianapolis, Ind.: The Society, 1972. 66 pp., illus. ◆ Scenes along the Wabash.

Indiana Junior Historical Society. *A View of Ecclesiastical Architecture in Cass County, Indiana.* Indianapolis: The Society, Society of Indiana Pioneers, 1972. 30 pp., illus.

Montgomery, Robert W. "History for Young People: Organizing a Junior Society," *History News,* 22:9 (September 1967), Technical Leaflet no. 44.

"The New Preservation and Yorkers," *The Yorker,* 31:2 (December 1972), pp. 7-8, 13-14.

Platt, Doris. "History for Young People: Projects and Activities," *History News,* 21:9 (September 1966), Technical Leaflet no. 38.

Platt, Doris, ed. "The Youthful Outlook," *History News,* January 1966-May 1976. ◆ Column on projects and activities of young people.

Platt, Doris. "The Youthful Outlook: Teenage Docent Program at Old Economy," *History News,* 27:8 (August 1972), p. 177.

"Preservation Features: Come—and Bring the Children," *Historic Preservation,* 14:1 (1962), pp. 4-25.

Schnabel, Harry H. "Junior Curators: The Pilgrim Hall Experiment," *History News,* 17:6 (April 1962), pp. 86-88.

Stagg, Brian L. "Today's Youth, Tomorrow's Heritage: Getting Young People Involved," *Historic Preservation,* 24:2 (April-June 1972), pp. 16-18.

Stewart, Milo. "The Fayetteville–Manlius Yorkers—Youthful Leaders in Local History,"

History News, 20:11 (November 1965), pp. 247-249.

"Students Preserve Appalachian Folkways as They Uncover History From the Hills," *History News*, 27:3 (March 1972), pp. 48-50. ◆ Describes Foxfire project.

Switzerland County Junior Historical Society. *An Architectural and Historical Survey of Switzerland County*. Vevay, Ind.: The Society, 1969. 36 pp., illus., maps.

Winstanley, Barbara R. *Children and Museums*. Oxford: International Publication Service, 1967. 125 pp., illus., bibliog.

NOTES

Listed below are a few well-established and active junior historian groups. The list is by no means complete and there are many more which have not been included. For an up-to-date list of groups and their activities in your area, contact your state historical society or state history department.

Jerseymen Program. Junior membership program of the New Jersey Historical Society, 230 Broadway, Newark, New Jersey 07104. Each student receives a subscription to the *Cockpit* plus a membership card, special student materials, and invitations to participate in conferences and contests. The club receives a charter and the opportunity to enter state Jerseymen activities.

Junior Historians of Texas. Junior membership organization of the Texas State Historical Association, Box 8059 University Station, Austin, Texas 78712. Ten students may form a chapter. They receive the *Junior Historian* magazine and a subscription to the *Southwestern Historical Quarterly*.

Northwest Trailblazers. Junior historians of the Oregon Historical Society, 1230 S.W. Park Avenue, Portland, Oregon 97205. Five or more junior historians may form a chapter. Membership includes a membership card, club charter and the quarterly magazine, *Discovery*.

Yorker Program. Junior membership organization of the New York State Historical Association, Cooperstown, New York 13326. With membership each student receives a subscription to *The Yorker*, a quarterly magazine, and free admission to the museums of the New York State Historical Association.

Children's Museums

"Children's Museum Section: All For the Sake of Children," *Museum News*, 46:7 (March 1968), pp. 30-36. ◆ Includes: David Abbey, "Kids, Kulture and Curiosity"; Michael Butler, "What Are We Teaching"; and Carroll L. Williams, "Head Strong for Head Start."

"Children's Museum Section: The Place of a Children's Museum in the Community," *Museum News*, 45:4 (December 1966), pp. 33-37. ◆ Includes: Russell Peithman, "The Place of a Children's Nature Museum in the Community"; Beatrice Parsons, "The Place of a Children's Museum in the Public Schools"; and W. Drew Check, Jr., "The Place of a Children's Museum as a Part of a Specialized Service."

"Children's Museum Section: What's in a Name?" *Museum News*, 45:9 (May 1967), pp. 32-36. ◆ Includes: Aalbert Heine, "Attendance, Population and the Junior Museum"; Philbrook Crouch, "How Does the Name 'Children's Museum' Affect Finances"; and Gloria Glossling, "A Children's Museum Changes Its Name."

Fisher, Helen V. "Children's Museums: A Definition and a Credo," *Curator*, III:2 (1960), pp. 183-191.

Gans, Susan. "Three Successful Programs Do Not a Museum Make," *Museum News*, 52:7 (April 1974), pp. 14-19. ◆ Examines the development of the Pittsburgh Children's Museum Project and the problems it encountered.

International Council of Museums. *Museums and Young People*. Paris: International Council of Museums, 1952. 131 pp. ◆ Articles by Germaine Cart, Molly Harrison, and Charles Russell. Available from ERIC Document Reproduction Service, Computer Microfilm International Corporation, P.O. Box 190, Arlington, Virginia 22210. ERIC # ED 046 233.

Marcousé, Reneé. "The Children's Museum, Boston, USA," *Museums' Annual: Education—Cultural Action*, 4 (1972), pp. 3-8.

Moore, Eleanor M. *Youth in Museums*. Philadelphia: University of Pennsylvania Press, 1941. 115 pp., illus. ◆ A survey of museum education activities based on visits to more than one hundred museums. May still be read with profit as an introduction to museum education. Out-of-print, available in some libraries.

Munro, Alan R. "The Yellow Submarine," *Museum News,* 46:6 (February 1968), pp. 20-23. ♦ Describes the mobile museum of the Children's Museum in Nashville, Tennessee.

Naumer, Helmuth J. "The Great Incorporation: The Youth Museum and Education." In *Museums and Education* (Washington, D.C.: Smithsonian Institution Press, 1968), pp. 129-137.

Parr, A. E. "Why Children's Museums?" *Curator,* III:3 (1960), pp. 217-236.

Wittlin, Alma S. "Junior Museums at the Crossroads: Forward to a New Era of Creativity or Backward to Obsoleteness?" *Curator,* VI:1 (1963), pp. 58-63.

NOTES

Directory of Youth Museum Programs. The American Association of Youth Museums has begun work on a comprehensive *Directory of Youth Museum Programs* throughout the United States. The directory will provide information on how to begin and operate children's museums and related institutions. The compilation is being carried out by Bonnie Pitman, Curator of Education, New Orleans Museum of Art, P.O. Box 19123, New Orleans, Louisiana 70179.

American Association of Youth Museums. An informal organization of directors and education department heads whose institutions have formal participatory activities for children. In addition, those youngsters account for at least seventy percent of the total number of participants. AAYM is affiliated with the American Association of Museums. Its purpose is to promote and improve the youth museum field and communications within the field. Contact: Adalie Brent, Director, Louisiana Arts and Science Center, 502 North Boulevard, Baton Rouge, Louisiana 70802.

Museum Programs for the Handicapped

Art Education for the Disadvantaged Child; *A Series of Six Articles Reprinted from the Pages of Art Education.* Edited by Doris

Barclay. Washington, D.C.: National Art Education Association, 1969. 30 pp., illus.

Bartlett, J. "Museums and the Blind," *Museums Journal,* 54:11 (February 1955), pp. 283-287.

Calhoun, Sallie N. "On the Edge of Vision," *Museum News,* 52:7 (April 1974), pp. 36-41.

Coon, Nelson. *The Place of the Museum in the Education of the Blind.* New York: American Federation for the Blind, 1953. 46 pp., illus.

Hellman, Robert, and Elizabeth Hellman. "A Nature Trail for the Blind," *Museum News,* 39:9 (June 1961), pp. 24-25.

Henriksen, Harry C. "Your Museum: A Resource for the Blind," *Museum News,* 50:2 (October 1971), pp. 26-28.

Hunter, C. Bruce. "A Summer Program for the Blind," *Curator,* I:3 (Summer 1968), pp. 43-47.

Kenney, Alice P. "Museums from a Wheelchair," *Museum News,* 53:4 (December 1974), pp. 14-17.

Moore, George. "Displays for the Sightless," *Curator,* XI:4 (1968), pp. 292-296. ♦ Discusses considerations inherent in preparing exhibitions for the blind which can apply to exhibition problems in general. See also: *Museums Journal,* 68:4 (March 1968), pp. 154-155.

Ricards, G. T. "Exhibitions for the Blind and Partially Blind," *Museums Journal,* 50:12 (March 1951), pp. 284-286.

Rowland, William. "Museums and the Blind," *ICOM News,* 26:3 (1973), pp. 117-119.

Stanford, Charles W., Jr. "The Mary Duke Biddle Gallery for the Blind," *Museums' Annual: Education—Cultural Action,* (1969), pp. 23-24.

Stanford, Charles W., Jr. "A Museum Gallery for the Blind," *Museum News,* 44:10 (June 1966), pp. 18-23.

"Tactile Mobile Museum," *Environment Southwest,* 411 (April 1969), n. p.

Watkins, Malcolm J. "A Small Handling Table for Blind Visitors," *Museums Journal,* 75:1 (June 1975), pp. 29-30.

NOTES

The Illinois State Museum, Spring and Edwards Streets, Springfield, Illinois 62706, publishes a monthly braille edition of its bulletin, *The Living Museum.*

The Mary Duke Biddle Gallery for the Blind, North Carolina Museum of Art, 107 East Morgan Street, Raleigh, North Carolina 27611, is designed to provide the blind visitor with an understanding of the history of art, through the use of three dimensional art objects. It also maintains a braille reference library in art history and publishes braille catalogues of the objects on exhibit.

The Philadelphia Museum of Art, Division of Education, 26th Street and Benjamin Franklin Parkway, Box 7646, Philadelphia, Pennsylvania 19101, conducts a program for the blind, "Form in Art," which seeks to translate the visual arts into a tangible reality through lectures on the history of art, emphasizing basic principles such as form, texture and size rela-tionships, combined with studio sculpture classes.

The San Diego Natural History Museum, P.O. Box 1390, San Diego, California 92112, operates a Tactile Mobile Museum for the blind, partially sighted, deaf and hard of hearing students in the city school system. Specimens are chosen so that children may feel, taste and smell exhibits, comparing weights, textures and sizes.

A Tactile Gallery, Wadsworth Atheneum, 600 Main Street, Hartford, Connecticut 06103, offers experiences in non-visual perception to both blind and sighted visitors.

The Touring Art Gallery for the Sighted and Blind was founded in 1970 by the California Arts Commission, 808 "O" Street, Sacramento, California 95814, as a public service for museums, galleries and citizens of the state.

5

Museums and Schools

School children constitute a very substantial percentage of the visitation to most museums, historic sites, and historical societies. As a result museum-school programs represent an important facet of the interpretive activities of these organizations. School services take many forms: school group tours, in-school visits by museum staff, role playing experiences for school children, production and distribution of loan kits, teacher training workshops, and the production and sale of curriculum materials. (See also sections on administering instructional media programs and audiovisual techniques in Chapter 7.) The wide variety of activities and materials are described in the references in this chapter, Museums and Schools.

The first section, Educational Theory, cites some basic references which may help the museum educators to understand the principles of teaching and learning which must be the basis for a successful museum-school program. Furthermore, familiarity with the current theories in the education field may facilitate communication with the teachers who play such a crucial role in the success or failure of a school program.

Museum-School Programs includes two sections, General References and Case Studies. Attention is given first to basic problems and issues involved in the museum-school relationship as well as surveys of school services in museums. Case Studies provides descriptions in some detail of specific school programs developed by historical societies and museums. Many of these also include an evaluation of the success or failure of the programs. Such information can be quite helpful to other museums in formulating their own school programs.

The last section, Museum Resources for Schools, lists publications which provide suggestions for how the school can use the museum and its resources or which are themselves museum–generated materials for use in the schools. Also listed are some representative sources for museum materials. Teachers should consult their own local and state historical societies and museums for local history materials. For a wider range of museum resources, consult Paul Wasserman's *Museum Media: A Biennial Directory and Index of Publications and Audiovisuals Available from United States and Canadian Institutions,* listed below.

Those involved in museum-school programs may also find some sections of Chapter 4 helpful. In particular, the sections on orientation programs, docents, guides and volunteers, children's museums, and junior programs include pertinent references.

36

Educational Theory

Ausubel, David P. *The Psychology of Meaningful Verbal Learning: An Introduction to School Learning.* New York: Grune and Stratton, 1963. 255 pp.

Ballard, Martin, ed. *New Movements in the Study and Teaching of History.* Bloomington, Ind.: Indiana University Press, 1970. 234 pp., bibliog. footnotes. ◆ Chapter on "The Teacher's Opportunities" suggests possible application of resources of museums and historic sites to teaching of history.

Baxter, Maurice G.; Robert H. Ferrell; and John E. Wiltz. *The Teaching of American History in High Schools.* Bloomington, Ind.: Indiana University Press, 1964. 160 pp. ◆ The authors concluded that most teachers they questioned lacked adequate knowledge of the subject and had little time to remedy this lack with reading.

Berger, Peter, and Thomas Luckmann. *The Social Construction of Reality: A Treatise in the Sociology of Knowledge.* Garden City, N.Y.: Doubleday, 1966. 203 pp., bibliog. ◆ This discussion of social processes that contribute to a sense of reality provides a conceptual framework for considering the "reality" which is so often attributed to museum objects.

Bruner, Jerome S. *On Knowing: Essays for the Left Hand.* Cambridge, Mass.: Harvard University Press, 1962. 165 pp. ◆ Ten essays centered around the theme of how we know and how knowledge reflects the structuring power of the human intellect, how we impart knowledge and teach the learner to construct his own world of learning.

Bruner, Jerome S. *The Process of Education.* Cambridge, Mass.: Harvard University Press, 1960. 97 pp. ◆ Thoughts growing out of a conference of scientists, scholars, and educators in 1959, discussing how science education might be improved in U.S. elementary and secondary schools.

Bruner, Jerome S. *Toward a Theory of Instruction.* Cambridge, Mass.: Harvard University Press, 1966. 176 pp.

Edling, Jack V. *Individualized Instruction: A Manual for Administrators.* Corvallis, Ore.: Continuing Education Publications, 1970. 137 pp., illus. ◆ Layman's survey of the many alternative ways to try to individualize instruction.

ERIC Clearinghouse on Media and Technology. *Museums and Media: A Status Report,* prepared by Richard Grove; and *Museums and Media: A Basic Reference Shelf,* by Philip C. Ritterbush. Stanford, Calif.: ERIC Clearinghouse on Educational Media and Technology at the Institute for Communication Research, Stanford University, 1970. 15 pp. ◆ Based on a paper prepared for the President's Commission on Instructional Technology in 1968. Bibliography lists books, papers, periodicals and reports to help show the important role museums play in elementary and secondary education.

Fenton, Edwin. *The New Social Studies.* New York: Holt, Rinehart & Winston, Inc., 1967. 144 pp., bibliog. footnotes.

Gage, N. L., ed. *Handbook of Research on Teaching; A Project of the American Educational Research Association.* Chicago: Rand-McNally, 1963. 1218 pp., illus. ◆ Contains reviews of psychological and educational research on the teaching process. The social background of teaching, the group interaction which occurs in the classroom and selected investigations on social studies teaching techniques are reviewed.

Ginsburg, Herbert, and Sylvia Opper. *Piaget's Theory of Intellectual Development; An Introduction.* Englewood Cliffs, N.J.: Prentice-Hall, 1969. 237 pp., illus., bibliog. footnotes.

Guilford, J. P., and Benjamin Fruchter. *Fundamental Statistics in Psychology and Education.* 5th ed. New York: McGraw-Hill Co., 1973. 605 pp., illus.

Holt, John C. *How Children Fail.* New York: Delta, 1970. 223 pp. ◆ Discusses what is wrong with education in American schools in the mid-1960's, how schools fail to meet the needs of children and makes distinctions between real and apparent learning.

Holt, John C. *How Children Learn.* New York: Pitman Publishing Corp., 1969. 189 pp. ◆ Observations and reflections on the ways of a child's mind as it develops into an effective instrument of learning.

Humanities and the Social Studies. Edited by Thomas F. Powell. Washington, D.C.: National Council for the Social Studies, 1969. 245 pp., bibliog. references. ◆ National Council for the Social Studies Bulletin no. 44.

Leonard, George B. *Education and Ecstasy.* New York: Delacorte Press, 1968. 239 pp.

Massialas, Byron G., and C. Benjamine Cox. *Inquiry in the Social Studies.* New York: McGraw-Hill, 1966. 353 pp., bibliog. ♦ Teaching of social studies using the inquiry method and critical thinking.

National Council for the Social Studies. *Index to NCSS Publications: A Topical Bibliography of Yearbooks, Bulletins, Curriculum Series and Articles in Social Education, June 1961-June 1969.* Compiled by Grace Kachaturoff. Washington, D.C.: The Council, 1970. 44 pp.

National Council for the Social Studies. *Interpreting and Teaching American History.* Edited by William H. Cartwright and Richard L. Watson. Washington, D.C.: The Council, 1965. 430 pp., bibliog. footnotes. ♦ National Council for the Social Studies 31st Yearbook.

National Council for the Social Studies. *Teaching American History: The Quest for Relevancy.* Edited by Allan O. Kownslar. Washington, D.C.: The Council, 1974. 237 pp., illus. ♦ National Council for the Social Studies 44th Yearbook.

"New Learning Spaces and Places," *Design Quarterly,* 90-91 (1974), entire issue. ♦ Describes various experiments in school architecture to develop more effective learning environments. An exhibition organized by Walker Art Center with the cooperation of the Minneapolis Public Schools, January 27-March 10, 1974.

Parr, Albert E. "Information, Vocabulary, Motivation and Memory," *Museum News,* 46:9 (May 1968), pp. 28-29. ♦ Discusses important factors involved in the learning process, as related to the museum setting.

Sobel, Harold W., and Arthur E. Salz. *The Radical Papers: Readings in Education.* New York: Harper & Row, 1972. 213 pp.

NOTES AND PERIODICALS

Learning; Magazine for Creative Teaching. 1972, 9/yr., subscription, tabloid format. Thomas O. Ryder, 530 University Avenue, Palo Alto, California 94301. ♦ Deals with the classroom teacher's problems and reviews books, new teaching techniques, the open classroom.

National Council for the Social Studies, 1201 16th Street, N.W., Washington, D.C. 20036. This organization has many publications available that would be of interest to museum educators working in the area of social studies. The purpose of the Council is "to promote the study of the problems of teaching the social studies to the best advantage of the students in the classroom." Publications include a journal, *Social Education; Yearbook;* and a monograph series on courses of study, classroom aids and test items.

National Council for the Social Studies, *Yearbook.* 1930, annual, membership. National Council for the Social Studies, 1201 16th Street, N.W., Washington, D.C. 20036. ♦ This is an important source for the latest ideas and developments in social studies teaching.

Research in Education. 1966, monthly, subscription. U.S. Government Printing Office, Washington, D.C. 20405. ♦ A publication of Educational Resources Information Center, National Center for Educational Communication, Office of Education, U.S. Department of Health, Education and Welfare. A journal of abstracts on recently completed research and research related reports and current research projects in the field of education. Reproductions of all documents cited in the "Document Resumé" are available from ERIC and information on ordering is included in each issue of the journal. This journal is best used in conjunction with *Thesaurus of ERIC Descriptors* which gives a clue to the ERIC system of information storage and retrieval.

Social Education. 1937, monthly (October-May), membership or subscription. National Council for the Social Studies, 1201 16th Street, N.W., Washington, D.C. 20036.

Museum–School Programs

General References

Benedict, Paul L. "Historic Site Interpretation: The Student Field Trip," *History News,* 26:3 (March 1971), Technical Leaflet no. 19.

Bloomberg, Marguerite. *An Experiment in Museum Instruction . . . Conducted at the Cleveland Museum of Art to Determine the Relative Effectiveness of Several Types of Museum Lessons for Children of Average and*

High Mentality. Washington, D.C.: American Association of Museums, 1929. 40 pp., illus. ◆ Photocopy available from ERIC Document Reproduction Service, Computer Microfilm International Corporation, P.O. Box 190, Arlington, Virginia 22210. ERIC # ED 044 921. The study is a comparison of the educational effectiveness of a variety of learning strategies in the Cleveland Museum of Art for groups of students ranked by their schools into different ability groups. It is a classical experimental study on varying methods of museum school tour instruction and arousing exploration behavior in children.

Coleman, Laurence Vail. "Educational Work." In *Manual for Small Museums* (New York: G. P. Putnam's Sons, 1927), pp. 241-290. ◆ Includes activities for children, school-service, adult education, the museum library, publications, and publicity.

"College and University Section: Views from Within," *Museum News,* 46:3 (November 1967), pp. 35-39. ◆ Includes: Paul Love, "The Kresge Art Center and the Michigan State University"; Irving Reiman, "The Role of a University Museum in the Education of Students and the Public."

"Education Section: The Museum's Role in Curriculum Development," *Museum News,* 45:6 (February 1967), pp. 34-39. ◆ Includes: Doris Platt, "A Contribution to Classroom History Study"; Miriam Wood, "A Museum's Contribution to Curriculum"; Evelyn Carlson, "Museum and Curriculum Development in Chicago."

"Education Section: Today's Problems and Implications for Museum Education," *Museum News,* 46:2 (October 1967), pp. 31-37. ◆ Includes: Ella Martin, "Why Museum Education in Today's World"; Lois Bark, "Museum Experience for the Exceptional Child"; Gilbert Merrill, "New Dimensions in Museum Teaching."

Evernham, Clark C. "Science Education: A Museum Responsibility," *Museum News,* 40:2 (October 1961), pp. 20-22. ◆ Discussion of the role of the educational staff in museums coupled with a plea for new ways to train educators for museums.

Frasch, Robert W. "Teacher Reactions to a Museum's Loan Service," *The Museologist,* 109 (December 1968), pp. 11-16.

Grove, Richard. "The Arts in Education," *The Museologist,* 115 (June 1970), pp. 4-11.

Harrison, Molly. *Changing Museums: Their Use and Misuse.* London: Longmans, Green & Co., Ltd., 1967. 110 pp., illus., bibliog.

Harrison, Molly. *Learning Out of School: A Teacher's Guide to the Educational Use of Museums.* Rev. ed. London: Ward Lock Educational, 1970. 80 pp., illus., bibliog.

Hayes, Bartlett H., Jr. *A Study of the Relation of Museum Art Exhibitions to Education.* Washington, D.C.: U.S. Department of Health, Education and Welfare, Office of Education, Bureau of Research, 1967. 54 pp., bibliog., appendix. ◆ Available from ERIC Document Reproduction Service, Computer Microfilm International Corporation, P.O. Box 190, Arlington, Virginia 22210. ERIC # ED 026 403. Reports on the practice of fifty-seven museums in various locations and offers recommendations for closer consultation between schools and art museums.

Hayes, Bartlett H., Jr. "A Study of the Relation of Museum Art Exhibitions to Education." In *Museums and Education* (Washington, D.C.: Smithsonian Institution Press, 1968), pp. 49-75.

International Council of Museums. Committee for Education. *Museums and Teachers.* Paris: The Council, 1956. 33 pp.

Long, Mary. "Priorities: School Loan Services and Visits to Museums," *Museums' Annual: Education—Cultural Action,* 4 (1972), pp. 9-11.

Melton, Arthur W.; Nita Goldberg Feldman; and Charles W. Mason. *Experimental Studies of the Education of Children in a Museum of Science.* Washington, D.C.: American Association of Museums, 1936. 111 pp. ◆ Available from ERIC Document Reproduction Service, Computer Microfilm International Corporation, P.O. Box 190, Arlington, Virginia 22210. ERIC # ED 044 927. Summarizes studies of learning conducted among children visiting the Buffalo Museum of Science, including evaluations of advanced preparation, illustrated lectures, and methods of instruction.

Moore, Eleanor M. *Youth in Museums.* Philadelphia: University of Pennsylvania Press, 1941. 115 pp., illus.

Museums Association. Group for Educational Services in Museums. *Museum School Services.* Prepared by the Group for Educational Services in Museums; edited by Francis W. Cheetham. London: Museums Association, 1967. 48 pp., illus., bibliog., appendices. ♦ Includes administration, local factors governing the organization of a museum school service, public relations, accommodations and equipment, staff, finance, teaching services, loan services.

Pitman, Bonnie L., ed. *Southeast Museums Conference Directory of Education Programs and Resources.* New Orleans: Southeast Museums Conference of the AAM, 1974. 162 pp., bibliog. ♦ Includes program descriptions of 86 institutions in the twelve state southeast region as well as education staff listings; a compendium of resource people and organizations with expertise in such areas as administration, community development, docent training and exhibitions; bibliography of publications in education, exhibits, media, etc., used by professionals. Available from Bonnie Pitman, Curator of Education, New Orleans Museum of Art, P.O. Box 19123, New Orleans, Louisiana 70179.

Robinson, E. S. "Experimental Education in the Museum—A Perspective," *Museum News,* 10:16 (1933), pp. 6-8. ♦ Outlines some ideas for helping museums experiment with their educational ideas. Suggests that museums systematically alter interior dimensions to achieve different effects on visitors.

Russell, Charles. *Museums and Our Children: A Handbook and Guide for Teachers in Museums and Schools for All Who Are Interested in Programs of Activity for Children.* New York: Central Book Co., 1956. 338 pp., illus. ♦ A practical guide filled with examples drawn from the programs of many museums.

Shotz, Sidney A. "Forming an Educational Alliance," *Museum News,* 40:7 (March 1962), pp. 30-32.

Stewart, Milo V. "The Museum and the School: Avenues to Collaboration," *The Museologist,* 110 (March 1969), pp. 11-13.

"A Survey: Museums and the Young," *Clés Pour Les Arts,* 22 (June 1972), pp. 20-28. ♦ English translation available from Les Amis des Musées Royaux des Beaux Arts, 9 Rue des Musées, Brussels. Describes education programs of the Brooklyn Museum, Boston Children's Museum, and Anacostia, as well as the general results of the survey based on questionnaires returned by forty-five museums.

Taylor, Anne P. "Children and Artifacts—A Replacement for Textbook Learning," *Curator,* XVI:1 (March 1973), pp. 25-29.

Williams, Patterson B. "Find Out Who Donny Is," *Museum News,* 52:7 (April 1974), pp. 42-45. ♦ Argues that although multiple-visit school programs are necessary in providing full educational services, museums should not forget the value of one-shot visits.

Youngpeter, John M. "Museum Field Trips—Enhancement Through Creative Planning," *Curator,* XVI:3 (September 1973), pp. 267-270.

Zuelke, Ruth. "Some Thoughts About Secondary Schools and Museums." In *Museums and Education* (Washington, D.C.: Smithsonian Institution Press, 1968), pp. 87-91.

NOTES

Museum Education Roundtable, 514 Tenth Street, Washington, D.C. 20005, is a nonprofit educational corporation whose members include a variety of professionals interested in furthering the use of cultural and scientific institutions as educational resources. Its concerns include museum-school cooperation, in-service training for museum educators on such subjects as the use of the media in the museum, docent training and evaluation.

Museums Collaborative, 830 Fifth Avenue, New York, New York 10021. Museums Collaborative has two goals: to assist museums in decentralizing their resources and in using these resources in novel ways to reach new audiences; to provide joint services to museum education departments including fund raising, publicity and information exchange. It is affiliated with the New York City Department of Cultural Affairs.

Case Studies

American Association for State and Local History. *Learning History Through Direct Experience: A Museum Program for Children.* Nashville, Tenn.: The Association, 1975. 11 minute tape cassette, slide carousel, supplementary material. Rental or purchase.

✦ Relates the experiences of a successful children's summer workshop program at Littleton Area (Colo.) Historical Museum. Includes a transcript of an interview with officials of the museum about the philosophy of the workshop.

Anderson, Duane C. "Creative Teaching, Temporary Exhibits, and Vitality for the Small Museum," *Curator,* XII:3 (September 1969), pp. 180-183. ✦ Describes a long-term temporary exhibition program at the Sanford Museum in Cherokee, Iowa.

Anderson, Duane C. "Project ETW: An Exemplary School–Museum Program," *Curator,* XVI:2 (June 1973), pp. 141-157. ✦ Includes sample lesson plans.

Bay, Ann. *Museum Programs for Young People.* Washington, D.C.: Smithsonian Institution, 1973. 282 pp., illus. ✦ Case studies of education programs in 14 American museums and discussion of programs of special interest.

Black, Patricia F. *The Live–In at Old Economy. An Experiment in a Role Playing Educational Program in the Museum.* Ambridge, Pa.: The Harmonie Associates, Inc., 1972. 42 pp., illus.

Bloch, Linda. "The Red Box: An Improvised Suitcase Exhibit," *Museum News,* 47:7 (March 1969), pp. 29-31. ✦ Describes a travelling exhibit, circulated to schools from the Little Rock Museum of Science and Natural History, intended to stimulate curiosity about natural objects.

Bloom, Joel N. "School Without Walls," *Museum News,* 50:2 (October 1971), pp. 18-20. ✦ Describes the Parkway Program in Philadelphia.

"Bringing Schools to Local History: The Braintree Historical Society," *History News,* 20:3 (March 1965), pp. 59-61.

Christison, Muriel. "The Design Game," *Museum News,* 50:3 (November 1971), pp. 16-17. ✦ Describes the use of kits of design elements (color, line, shapes, textures) to study works of art with children.

Cleveland Museum of Art. *Educational Work at the Cleveland Museum of Art.* By Thomas Munro and Jane Grimes. 2nd ed., rev. Cleveland: Cleveland Museum of Art, 1952. 89 pp., illus.

Cook, Anne H., and Jane T. Breinholt. *Project 1776: A Manual for the Bicentennial.* Rev. ed. Devon, Pa.: Pennsylvania Bicentennial Commission, 1974. 206 pp., illus., bibliog. ✦ A source book of history and learning ideas in Early American Culture for elementary school pupils.

"Crafts Link Historical Societies to School," *History News,* 29:9 (September 1974), p. 220. ✦ Describes a project by Stark County Historical Center (Ohio) to bring craft demonstrations to schools.

Danilov, Victor J. "Under the Microscope," *Museum News,* 52:6 (March 1974), pp. 37-44. ✦ A close examination of educational programs in fifteen science museums reveals the range and variety of approaches to science education.

Dennis, Emily. "Grant Material: A Museum Program in Anthropology and Archaeology for High School Students," *Museum News,* 45:6 (February 1967), pp. 13-16. ✦ Describes direct student participation in the study of field sites near the Brooklyn Children's Museum with the support of the National Science Foundation.

"A Do-It-Yourself Adventure in Learning at Old Sturbridge Village," *The Museologist,* 117 (December 1970), pp. 19-22. ✦ Describes school programs at the "Discovery Center" at Old Sturbridge Village.

Great Britain. Department of Education and Science. *Museums in Education.* London: Her Majesty's Stationery Office, 1971. 55 pp., illus. ✦ Survey of educational services of eight British museums, including loan services, lecture services, teaching, adult education.

Group for Educational Services in Museums. *Museum Education Services.* Museums Association Information Sheet no. 1. 2nd ed. London: Museums Association, 1972. 4 pp.

Hart, Bernard F. "Using the Artifact Outside the Exhibit," *CMA Gazette,* 4:4-5 (August-November 1970), pp. 11-13. ✦ Describes a school loan program and teacher workshops at the Nova Scotia Museum.

"Heritage Workshop Reflects Enthusiasm of Young People for Early American Crafts," *History News,* 27:1 (January 1972), pp. 30-31. ✦ Describes a program at the Clinton (N.J.) Historical Museum.

Humbert, Aimée, and France Lerondeau. "An Experiment with Loan Material," *Museums' Annual: Education—Cultural Action,* no. 4 (1972), pp. 11-14.

Kirk, Irving D. "Communication: The Museum and the School," *Museum News,* 42:9 (May 1964), pp. 18-20. ◆ The museum teacher for the School District of Philadelphia at the Franklin Institute explains how communication breakdown occurs and what can be done about it.

Kresse, Frederick H. *Materials and Activities for Teachers and Children: A Project to Develop and Evaluate Multi-Media Kits for Elementary Schools.* 2 vols. Washington, D.C.: U.S. Department of Health, Education and Welfare, Office of Education, Bureau of Research, 1968. ◆ Available from ERIC Document Reproduction Service, Computer Microfilm International Corporation, P.O. Box 190, Arlington, Virginia 22210. ERIC # ED 033 615-5. Volume I describes the objectives, methods and findings of the MATCH Project at the Boston Children's Museum, a four year program conducted to demonstrate and explore the characteristics of self-contained, multi-media kits designed to enable elementary teachers and children to communicate by non-verbal means. Volume II contains analysis and evaluation of the project and includes appendices containing sample evaluation forms, portions of individual box reports, sample pages from teachers' guides, and examples of tabulated data from second generation boxes.

Levy, Virginia. "Museum to Classroom," *Museum News,* 47:4 (December 1968), pp. 22-23. ◆ Discusses slide lectures brought to the schools by visiting volunteers from the museum.

Love, Becky. *Ideals from History.* Littleton, Colo.: Children's Summer Workshop, 1972. 42 pp., illus. ◆ Describes an internship program with aid from NEH and other groups.

McLanathan, Richard. "Art and Man: Extending Museum Resources," *Museum News,* 49:2 (October 1970), pp. 18-20. ◆ The National Gallery of Art has devised a multi-media program entitled *Art and Man* aimed at the junior and senior high school level. It consists of eight monthly packages, each devoted to a basic theme scheduled from October to May to coincide with the school year.

"Museums and Schools," *Midwest Museums Conference Quarterly,* 16:2 (April 1956), entire issue. ◆ Describes museum school programs at forty-three midwestern museums.

New York (State). Curriculum Development Center. *Schools and Museums; A Report on the School-Museum Cooperative Education Project.* Albany: State Education Department, 1968. 31 pp., illus. ◆ A concise summary of joint school-museum activities and program relationships. Out-of-print.

Powel, Lydia. *The Art Museum Comes to the School.* New York: Harper and Bros., 1944. 160 pp. ◆ Critical review of a cooperative program conducted by five museums and their school systems in New York.

Rabinowitz, Richard. "Museum Education at Old Sturbridge Village," *Museums' Annual: Education—Cultural Action,* 5 (1973), pp. 19-24.

Silver, Adele Z. "Education in a Museum: A Conservative Adventure," *Curator,* XV:1 (March 1972), pp. 72-85. ◆ Describes education programs at the Cleveland Museum of Art.

"A Survey: Museums and the Young," *Clés Pour Les Arts,* 22 (June 1972), pp. 20-28. ◆ English translation available from Les Amis des Musées Royaux des Beaux Arts, 9 Rue des Musées, Brussels. Describes education programs of the Brooklyn Museum, Boston Children's Museum, and Anacostia, as well as the general results of the survey based on questionnaires returned by forty-five museums.

Taylor, Jonathan. "High Schools, Inner Cities, Museums," *Curator,* XV:2 (June 1972), pp. 153-160. ◆ Describes a program at the Field Museum where high school students build exhibits which are sent to high schools.

Thomas, Marian. "The Community School Programme," *Museum News,* 47:4 (December 1968), pp. 19-21. ◆ Discusses methods of developing visual awareness in children of varying backgrounds.

Ward, Mary Sam. "Henry Clay Day: The Ultimate Field Trip," *Museum News,* 50:2 (October 1971), pp. 34-37. ◆ Describes an experiment in dimensional learning conducted by Hagley Museum and Mt. Pleasant School District in Wilmington, Delaware. It is an example of museum-school-library cooperation.

"Washington State Institutes Program for High School History Students," *History News*, 28:10 (October 1973), p. 226.

NOTES

Project 1776: A Bicentennial Program in Early American Culture for Elementary School Pupils. The purpose of Project 1776 is to enrich the social studies curriculum, specifically in colonial history, by recreating through sensory experiences the mood and life style that prevailed among the people at the time of our country's beginnings. It includes three phases: (1) in-service training for teachers, (2) demonstrations and related displays in schools using museum objects, (3) a field trip to an 18th-century Pennsylvania farm where they live as children of 1776. It is supported by the Bicentennial Commission of Pennsylvania and the Commissioners of Chester County with the sponsorship of the Chester County Historical Society.

Museum Resources for Schools

Bamford, Peter. "Original Sources in the Classroom." In *New Movements in the Study and Teaching of History* (Bloomington, Ind.: Indiana University Press, 1970), pp. 205-214. ◆ Discusses use of historical sites, manuscripts, graveyards, newspapers.

Cole, Anne Kilborn. *Old Things for Young People: A Guide to Antiques.* New York: David McKay Co., Inc., 1963. 174 pp., illus.

Cook, Anne H., and Jane T. Breinholt. *Project 1776: A Manual for the Bicentennial.* Rev. ed. Devon, Pa.: Pennsylvania Bicentennial Commission, 1974. 206 pp., illus., bibliog. ◆ A source book of history and learning ideas in Early American Culture for elementary school pupils.

Directory of Educational Opportunities in the Washington Area. 3rd ed. Edited by Mary S. Alexander. Washington, D.C.: Museum Education Roundtable, 1973. 48 pp. ◆ Lists approximately eighty basic resources, including museums, libraries, nature centers and historical sites and houses, as well as government agencies and departments which are open to the public.

ERIC Clearinghouse on Media and Technology. *Museums and Media: A Status Report,* prepared by Richard Grove: and *Museums and Media: A Basic Reference Shelf,* by Philip C. Ritterbush. Stanford, Calif.: ERIC Clearinghouse on Educational Media and Technology at the Institute for Communication Research, Stanford University, 1970. 15 pp. ◆ Based on a paper prepared for the President's Commission on Instructional Technology in 1968. Bibliography lists books, papers, periodicals and reports to help show the important role museums play in elementary and secondary education.

Field Museum of Natural History. *Field Trip: A Museum Idea Book.* Chicago: Field Museum of Natural History, Department of Education, 1974. 26 pp.

Frasch, Robert W. "History Along New York Highways." Reprinted from *New York State Education,* February 1965. 3 pp., illus. ◆ An architectural primer. Available from Fenimore Book Store, New York State Historical Association, Cooperstown, New York 13326.

Georgia Heritage: Documents of Georgia History, 1730-1790. Prepared by the Georgia Department of Archives and History. Atlanta, Ga.: Georgia Commission for the National Bicentennial Celebration, 1973. ◆ Document facsimiles with descriptive text in a portfolio.

Hausman, Jerome J. *The Museum and the Art Teacher.* Final Report, December 1966. Washington, D.C.: George Washington University and National Gallery of Art, 1966. 30 pp., illus. ◆ A report on a summer workshop at the National Gallery of Art on the use of museum materials in the teaching of art at the secondary school level. It emphasizes the importance of a historical and technical perspective and includes a description of projects developed for student art classes by the participants.

Hertzberg, Hazel W. *The Great Tree and the Longhouse: The Culture of the Iroquois.* New York: MacMillan, 1966. 122 pp., illus. ◆ Produced by the Anthropology Curriculum Study Project. It is an excellent example of imaginative presentation of a culture, readily illustrated with museum objects.

Hertzberg, Hazel W. *Teacher's Manual for the Great Tree and the Longhouse: The Culture of the Iroquois.* New York: American Anthropological Association, 1967. 64 pp.

Hertzberg, Hazel W. *Teaching a Pre-Columbian Culture; The Iroquois.* Albany: University of the State of New York, State Education Department, Bureau of Secondary Curriculum Development, 1966. 77 pp., illus., bibliog. ✦ A guide unit for seventh grade social studies.

Janowitz, Gayle. *Helping Hands; Volunteer Work in Education.* Chicago: University of Chicago Press, 1966. 125 pp., bibliog. notes. ✦ A report on volunteer efforts to create out-of-school supplementary study centers.

Lord, Clifford, ed. *Localized History Series.* New York: Columbia University Teachers College College Press, 1964-71. ✦ A paperback series of *Students Guides to Localized History*. Includes individual states, cities, regions, and ethnic groups.

Lord, Clifford L. *Teaching History with Community Resources.* 2nd ed. New York: Teachers College, Columbia University, Bureau of Publications, 1967. 85 pp., bibliog. footnotes. ✦ Gives many suggestions for class projects using community resources, including museums.

Marriott, Alice. *Kiowa Years: A Study in Culture Impact.* New York: Macmillan, 1968. 173 pp., illus., bibliog. ✦ Produced by the Anthropology Curriculum Study Project, with a teacher's guide also available. Museum materials might be programmed to supplement this kind of presentation.

"Match Boxes," *American Education,* 3:1 (December 1966-January 1967), p. 9. ✦ Describes a project at the Boston Children's Museum.

Muessig, Raymond H., ed. *Social Studies Curriculum Improvement: A Guide for Local Communities.* Washington, D.C.: National Council for the Social Studies, 1965. 117 pp., bibliog. references. ✦ National Council for the Social Studies Bulletin no. 36.

Muscogee County School District and Columbus Museum of Arts and Crafts, Inc. *Experiences in Living History. Teacher's Guide.* Columbus, Ga.: Muscogee County School District, 1972. 124 pp., illus., bibliog., appendices.

National Archives and Records Service. *Documents from America's Past: Reproductions of Historical Documents in the National Archives.* Washington, D.C.: U.S. Government Printing Office, 1973. 22 pp., illus.

New York (State). Bureau of Industrial Arts Education. *Industrial Arts Museum Resources: A Directory of Selected Centers.* Albany: Bureau of Industrial Arts Education, 1971. 44 pp.

New York (State). Bureau of Secondary Curriculum Development. *Teaching the Age of the City: The Gilded Age and After (1865-1914): A Guide for Seventh Grade Social Studies . . . .* Text by Hazel Hertzberg. Albany: State Education Department, 1968. 131 pp., illus., bibliog.

New York (State). Bureau of Secondary Curriculum Development. *Teaching the Age of Homespun: A Guide for Seventh Grade Social Studies.* Text by Hazel Hertzberg. Albany: New York State Bureau of Secondary Curriculum Development, 1965. 84 pp., illus., bibliog.

Porter, Willis P. "Teacher Preparation for Better Use of Museum Resources," *Educational Leadership,* 11:5 (February 1954), pp. 300-305.

Rath, Frederick L., Jr. "The Museum in the Humanities," *Museum News,* 46:4 (December 1967), pp. 18-23.

"Teaching About the American Revolution: Material for Students," *Social Education,* 39:2 (February 1974), entire issue. ✦ Includes: "Exploring American Communities Past and Present," "Dealing with Conflict—the Element of Personal Choice," "Examining American Values."

Trogler, George C. *Beginning Experiences in Architecture: A Guide for the Elementary School Teacher.* New York: Van Nostrand Reinhold Co., 1972. 143 pp., illus., bibliog. ✦ How to explain space and structure to children.

Wasserman, Paul, ed. *Museum Media: A Biennial Directory and Index of Publications and Audiovisuals Available from United States and Canadian Institutions.* Detroit: Gale Research Co., 1973. 455 pp. ✦ Intended to provide bibliographic control of books, booklets, monographs, catalogs, pamphlets and leaflets, films and filmstrips, and other media which are prepared and distributed by museums, art galleries and related institutions in the U.S. and Canada. Biennial publication is planned.

Yellow Pages of Learning Resources; Resources Directory Area Code 800. Written by George Borowsky, et al. Edited by Richard Saul Wurman. Cambridge, Mass.: The MIT Press, 1972. 94 pp., illus. ◆ Lists alphabetically by subject matter all of the general types of learning resources and facilities in a typical city. Aimed at teaching people how to use their communities as a schoolhouse.

NOTES, PERIODICALS AND CATALOGS

Boston Children's Museum, Jamaicaway, Boston, Massachusetts 02130. The Boston Children's Museum has MATCH Box units available for loan or sale in fifteen subjects. MATCH units (Materials and Activities for Teachers and Children) are self-contained multi-media kits containing three dimensional objects and related films, photographs, recordings, games, guides, projectors, etc. Their purpose is to encourage non-verbal communication between teacher and class and to involve children in a variety of activities as agents of their own learning. They cover primarily elementary school social studies topics and are packaged in compartmented corrugated cardboard suitcases. Teachers Guides to MATCH Box units are available from ERIC Document Reproduction Service.

Colonial Williamsburg, AV Distribution Section, Box C, Williamsburg, Virginia 23185. *Films, Filmstrips, Records, Slides on Early American Life.*

Educators Guide to Free Social Studies Materials. 1961, annual, subscription. Educators Progress Service, Inc., Randolph, Wisconsin 53956.

Free and Inexpensive Learning Materials. 1941, biennial. George Peabody College for Teachers, Division of Survey and Field Services, Nashville, Tennessee 37203.

Multi-Media Kit on the 1930's. Ontario Institute for Studies in Education, 252 Bloor Street West, Toronto 5, Ontario, Canada. A secondary level assortment of filmstrips, tapes, records, pictures, stamps, etc., relating to life in North America in the 1930's.

National Gallery of Art, Extension Services, Washington, D.C. 20565. *Extension Service Catalog.* Lists films, filmstrips, and slide lectures available to schools, colleges, universities, libraries, museums or community groups free of charge except for transportation costs.

New York Metropolitan Museum of Art, Slide Library, Fifth Avenue and 82nd Street, New York, New York 10028. *Sources of Slides: The History of Art.* Contains an accumulated listing of sources where slides relevant to the history of art can be acquired.

New York State Historical Association, Education Department, Cooperstown, New York 13326. *Educational Services and Materials: Catalog.*

Old Sturbridge Village, Sturbridge, Massachusetts 01566. *Guide to Resources.* Includes itemization of actual documents included in the data bank resource packets and a bibliography of secondary sources. Also provides suggestions for classroom activities.

Project 1776: A Bicentennial Program in Early American Culture for Elementary School Pupils. The purpose of Project 1776 is to enrich the social studies curriculum, specifically in colonial history, by recreating through sensory experiences the mood and life style that prevailed among the people at the time of our country's beginnings. It includes three phases: (1) in-service training for teachers, (2) demonstrations and related displays in schools using museum objects, (3) a field trip to an 18th century Pennsylvania farm where students live as children of 1776. It is supported by the Bicentennial Commission of Pennsylvania and the Commissioners of Chester County with the sponsorship of the Chester County Historical Society.

University of California, Slide Room, Art Department, Santa Barbara, California 93106. *A Handlist of Museum Sources for Slides and Photographs.*

"Your Portable Museum," Slide and Film Service of the American Crafts Council, Research and Education Department, 44 West 53rd Street, New York, New York 10019. More than eighty color slide kits documenting craft exhibitions at the Museum of Contemporary Crafts and other museums are available for rent or purchase. Each set contains between sixteen and 140 slides with accompanying literature. Also available are a limited number of 35mm filmstrips with descriptive notes (for purchase only) and 16mm rental films.

6

Museum Exhibits

For better or worse, first impressions tend to be lasting and most visitors gain their first impression of a museum or historical society from its exhibits. Good exhibits can be an attraction to bring people into your museum and keep them coming back. Poor exhibits can discourage visitors from exploring the museum's resources any further. Therefore, it is important that museums put on their best face in their exhibits and create displays which are attractive, informative, and interesting.

In this chapter the user will find references which will help him cope with virtually any kind of exhibit problem, the theory and principles of exhibit design as well as some very practical how-to-do-it advice. The first section, Philosophy and Principles of Museum Exhibits, covers a wide range of issues: the role of exhibits in the overall museum program; the pros and cons of audiovisual techniques in exhibits; principles of visual communication; the relationship of learning to exhibits. The next section, Design Aspects, addresses itself to the basic principles of design and visual perception which must be considered in creating effective exhibits. Following a section on general techniques, Technical Aspects of Museum Exhibits deals with two special areas of exhibit construction. Exhibit Problems includes case exhibit design, the particular characteristics of temporary and travelling exhibits, the display of costumes, and other problems. Exhibit Techniques covers those skills which are essential to effective exhibits: lighting, labels, use of color, construction, and other techniques.

In addition to references on the design and construction of exhibits, three other sections are included which will be helpful in the overall exhibit program. Exhibits and Conservation offers a few references which will, hopefully, prevent the exhibit designer from endangering the well-being of the artifacts used in exhibits. For a more complete treatment of this subject, the reader should consult Volume 2 of *A Bibliography on Historical Organization Practices: Care and Conservation of Collections.* Exhibit Descriptions provides references which describe a variety of exhibits done in the past. Exhibit technicians may benefit from the experience of others.

Finally, Exhibit Evaluation may be the most important of all. For, if one cannot step back and objectively evaluate the final exhibit product, improvement is unlikely, if not impossible. References in this section include discussions of the need for standards and criteria for judging exhibits, techniques for evaluating their effectiveness and actual exhibit reviews.

Special and technical journals and sources of services and materials have been noted throughout the chapter.

Philosophy and Principles of Museum Exhibits

Alexander, Edward P. "Artistic and Historical Period Rooms," *Curator*, VII:4 (1964), pp. 263-281.

Brawne, Michael. *The New Museum: Architecture and Display.* New York: Frederick A. Praeger, Publishers, 1966. 208 pp., illus., drawings, diagrams, graphs, bibliog., index of architects. ◆ Presents broad overview of the relationship of architecture and display in museums selected from around the world.

Burcaw, G. Ellis. "Films for Teaching Museology: A Guide to Where They Are," *Museum News*, 46:3 (November 1967), pp., 25-26. ◆ Describes a variety of films on museum exhibitions.

Cruxent, J. M. "A Few Comments on Museumology: Display and the Visitor," *The Museologist*, 59 (June 1956), pp. 16-18. ◆ States that the barrier between visitor and display resulting from the showcase idea must be eliminated.

Dandridge, Frank. "The Value of Design in Visual Communication," *Curator*, IX:4 (December 1966), pp. 331-336. ◆ Supports the evidence showing that the design of a display can make a significant difference to the educational function of an exhibit. A number of variables, such as eye movement, kind of typesetting, use of peripheral vision, etc., are reviewed in relation to exhibit design.

Dubos, Rene. "Sensory Perception and the Museum Experience," *Museum News*, 52:2 (October 1973), pp. 50-51.

"Effective Exhibits—A Search for New Guidelines," *Museum News*, 46:5 (January 1968), pp. 37-45.

Fine, Paul A. "The Role of Design in Educational Exhibits," *Curator*, VI:1 (1963), pp. 37-44.

Gabus, Jean. "Aesthetic Principles and General Planning of Educational Exhibits," *Museum*, XVIII:1 (1965), pp. 2-59.

Guthe, Carl E. *So You Want a Good Museum: A Guide to the Management of Small Museums.* 1957. Reprint. Washington, D.C.: American Association of Museums, 1967. 37 pp.

Hall, Edward T. *The Hidden Dimension.* 1st ed. Garden City, N.Y.: Doubleday, 1966. 201 pp., illus., bibliog. ◆ Considers social and personal space and man's perception of it.

Hall, Edward T. *The Silent Language.* Garden City, N.Y.: Doubleday, 1973. 240 pp., illus., bibliog. ◆ A survey of reactions to spatial situations.

Hayes, Bartlett H., Jr. "A Study of the Relation of Museum Art Exhibitions to Education." In *Museums and Education* (Washington, D.C.: Smithsonian Institution Press, 1968), pp. 49-75.

"History Section: History Exhibits—The Path Ahead," *Museum News*, 46:10 (June 1968), pp. 31-34.

Joint Artists—Museums Committee. *The Museum and the Artist; Principles and Procedures Recommended by the Joint Artists-Museums Committee.* New York: American Federation of Arts, 1958. 30 pp.

Leavitt, Thomas W. "Meaning in Exhibition Programs," *Museum News*, 42:6 (February 1964), pp. 17-19.

"Museum Exhibition Philosophy," *Midwest Museums Conference Quarterly*, 14:2 (April 1954), entire issue.

Neal, Arminta. "Function of Display: Regional Museums," *Curator*, VIII:3 (1965), pp. 228-234.

Parr, Albert E. "Designed for Display," *Curator*, II:4 (1959), pp. 313-334.

Parr, Albert E. "Marketing the Message," *Curator*, XII:2 (June 1969), pp. 77-82. ◆ Discusses the philosophy governing exhibit designs and supports the idea of nonspecific multi-variable stimulation.

Parr, Albert E. "The Obsolescence and Amortization of Permanent Exhibits," *Curator*, V:3 (1962), pp. 258-264.

Parr, Albert E. "Patterns of Progress in Exhibition," *Curator*, V:4 (1962), pp. 329-345.

Ramsey, Margaret A. "Learning and Exhibits: Space for Learning," *Museum News*, 52:6 (March 1974), pp. 49-51. ◆ Space is a crucial factor to be considered in revitalizing museums.

Sampson, Richard A. "The Role of the

Museum Administrator in an Exhibit Program," *Midwest Museums Conference Quarterly,* 25:2 (Spring 1965), pp. 5-6.

Schaeffer, Margaret W. M. "The Display Function of the Small Museum," *Curator,* VIII:2 (1965), pp. 103-118.

"Science Technical Section: Effective Exhibits—A Search for New Guidelines," *Museum News,* 46:5 (January 1968), pp. 37-45.

Screven, Chandler G. "The Application of Programed Learning and Teaching Systems Procedures for Instruction in a Museum Environment." In *The Museum Visitor: Selected Essays and Surveys on Visitor Reaction to Exhibits in the Milwaukee Public Museum* (Milwaukee: Milwaukee Public Museum, 1969), pp. 167-174. ◆ Describes a project to adapt the basic features and methods of programed instruction and reinforcement theory to improve the instructional efficiency of museum exhibits.

Screven, Chandler G. "Learning and Exhibits: Instructional Design," *Museum News,* 52:5 (January-February 1973), pp. 67-75. ◆ An examination of instructional communication in designing exhibits.

Sewell, Davis St. A. "Building a Program Around the Exhibit," *CMA Gazette,* 4:4-5 (August-November 1970), pp. 26-28.

Shannon, Joseph. "The Icing is Good, But the Cake is Rotten," *Museum News,* 52:5 (January-February 1974), pp. 28-35. ◆ Decries the adulteration of museum exhibits with audio-visual technology.

Shettel, Harris H. "Exhibits: Art Form or Education Medium?" *Museum News,* 52:1 (September 1973), pp. 32-41. ◆ Discusses the need for museums to make use of modern educational technology to communicate intelligibly with visitors. Outlines the author's research on exhibit effectiveness and offers recommendations on upgrading didactic exhibits.

Sohl, Stanley. "Effective Exhibits," *The Museologist,* 112 (September 1969), pp. 17-26.

Swinton, William E. "Communicating with the Museum Visitor," *The Museologist,* 92 (September 1964), pp. 4-12.

Visual Communications Conference, 3rd, New York, 1958. *Creativity: An Examination of the Creative Process.* A Report on the Third Communications Conference of the Art Directors Club of New York. New York: Hastings House Publishers, 1959. 210 pp., illus.

Visual Communications Conference, 5th, New York, 1960. *Visual Communications: International.* A Report on the Fifth Communications Conference of the Art Directors Club of New York. New York: Hastings House Publishers, 1961. 160 pp., illus.

Wilson, Kenneth M. "A Philosophy of Museum Exhibition," *Museum News,* 46:2 (October 1967), pp. 13-19.

Wittlin, Alma S. "Exhibits: Interpretive, Under Interpretive, Misinterpretive—Absolutes and Relative Absolutes in Exhibit Techniques." In *Museums and Education* (Washington, D.C.: Smithsonian Institution Press, 1968), pp. 95-114.

Wittlin, Alma S. "Hazards of Communication by Exhibits," *Curator,* XIV:2 (June 1971), pp. 138-150.

Design Aspects of Museum Exhibits

Arnheim, Rudolph. *Art and Visual Perception: A Psychology of the Creative Eye.* Berkeley: University of California Press, c1954, 1969. 408 pp., illus., bibliog. ◆ Describes general principles (balance, shape, form, growth, space, light, color, movement) which could be useful in the design facet of exhibits.

Arnheim, Rudolph. *Visual Thinking.* Berkeley: University of California Press, 1969. 345 pp., illus., bibliog.

Barber, Bruce T. *Designer's Dictionary.* Lockport, N.Y.: The Upson Co., 1974. 416 pp., illus., index. ◆ Oriented toward commercial display but a good source for adaptable ideas.

Bayer, Herbert. "Aspects of Design of Exhibitions and Museums," *Curator,* IV:3 (1961), pp. 257-287.

Bernard, Frank J. *Dynamic Display, Technique and Practice.* Cincinnati: Display Publishing Company, 1956. 164 pp., illus.

Black, Misha, ed. *Exhibition Design.* London: Architectural Press, 1950. 186 pp., illus.

Bleicher, Edward. "Presentational Esthetics," *Museums News,* 46:2 (October 1967), pp. 20-23.

Bloch, Milton. "Improvised Exhibit Design for the Small Budget," *Museum News,* 47:1 (September 1968), pp. 21-24.

Brady, Cyrus Townsend, Jr. "The Designing of Purposeful Photographic Shows," *Curator,* II:2 (1959), pp. 129-136.

Buckley, Jim. *The Drama of Display; Visual Merchandising and its Techniques.* New York: Pellegrini and Cudahy, 1953. 224 pp., illus.

Dreyfuss, Henry. *Designing for People.* New York: Viking Press, 1973. 240 pp., illus.

Garrett, Lillian. *Visual Design: A Problem Solving Approach.* New York: Reinhold Publishing Corp., 1967. 215 pp., illus., bibliog.

Gregory, R. L. *Eye and Brain: The Psychology of Seeing.* 2nd ed. New York: McGraw Hill, 1973. 255 pp., illus., bibliog.

Hall, Pauline. *Display: The Vehicle for the Museum's Message.* Toronto: Historical Branch, Department of Public Records and Archives, 1969. 12 pp., illus., plan.

Lohse, Richard P. *New Design in Exhibitions; 75 Examples of the New Form of Exhibitions.* New York: Praeger, 1954. 260 pp., illus., plans.

Luckiesh, M. *Visual Illusions; Their Causes, Characteristics, and Applications.* New York: Dover Publications, 1965. 252 pp., illus., bibliog.

Marshall, W. E. "Adaptibility in Exhibition Design," *Museum News,* 39:2 (October 1960), pp. 33-35.

Miller, Leon G. "The Industrial Designer: New Member of the Museum Team," *Curator,* VI:2 (1963), pp. 187-190.

Moseley, Spencer; Pauline Johnson; and Hazel Koenig. *Crafts Design: An Illustrated Guide.* Belmont, Calif.: Wadsworth Publishing Co., 1962. 436 pp., illus., bibliog.

Nelms, Henning. *Thinking With a Pencil.* New York: Barnes and Noble, Inc., 1964. 347 pp., illus., maps, diagrams, bibliog.

Panero, Julius. *Anatomy for Interior Designers.* 3rd ed. New York: Whitney League of Designers, 1962. 146 pp., illus., diagrams, tables.

Parr, A. E. "Remarks on Layout, Display, and Response to Design," *Curator,* VII:2 (1964), pp. 131-142. ◆ Makes suggestions for museum exhibits techniques taken from commercial store displays.

Rattenbury, Arnold. *Exhibition Design: Theory and Practice.* New York: Van Nostrand Reinhold, 1971. 96 pp., illus., plans.

Schuldes, W.K.F. "Basic Principles of Exhibition Design," *Curator,* X:1 (March 1967), pp. 49-53.

Sutnar, Ladislav. *Visual Design in Action: Principles, Purposes.* New York: Hastings House, 1961. 1 vol. (unpaged), illus.

PERIODICALS

Design Quarterly. 1946, quarterly, subscription. Walker Art Center, 807 Hennepin Avenue, Minneapolis, Minnesota 55403.

Industrial Design: Designing for Industry. 1954, 10 issues per year, subscription. Whitney Publications, Inc., 130 East 59th Street, New York, New York 10022.

Interiors. 1888, monthly, subscription. Whitney Publications, Inc., 130 East 59th Street, New York, New York 10022.

Visual Merchandising. 1922, monthly, subscription. Signs of the Times Publishing Co., 407 Gilbert Avenue, Cincinnati, Ohio 45202. Formerly *Display World.*

Technical Aspects of Museum Exhibits

General Techniques

Adams, P. R. "The Exhibition." In *The Organization of Museums: Practical Advice* (Paris: UNESCO, 1960), pp. 126-145. ◆ Includes planning the exhibition, temporary exhibitions, labels, lighting, case design, mounting objects, and the travelling exhibition.

American Association of Museums. Environmental Committee. *Museums and the En-*

vironment: A Handbook for Education. New York: Arkville Press, 1971. 261 pp., illus. ♦ A guide for museums, historical societies, schools and colleges interested in initiating exhibits and other educational projects dealing with human ecology.

Beazley, Elizabeth. *The Countryside on View: A Handbook on Countryside Centres, Field Museums and Historic Buildings Open to the Public.* London: Constable and Company, Ltd., 1971. 207 pp., illus., plans, bibliog., index. ♦ Includes an extensive chapter on display.

Borhegyi, Stephan F. de. "Visual Communication in the Science Museum," *Curator,* VI:1 (1963), pp. 45-57. ♦ Discusses the programming of visual communication, with reference to convincing and effective exhibits on anthropology. Stresses the importance of sound, touch, and spatial setting.

Bowditch, George. *Basic Exhibit Techniques.* Nashville, Tenn.: American Association for State and Local History, 1973. 25 minute tape cassette, slide carousel, and supplementary materials. Rental or purchase. ♦ Examines the many danger spots that beginning exhibit preparators tend to forget. Discusses the efficient use of space, open exhibits security, color, labeling, and arrangement of artifacts.

Bowditch, George, and Holman J. Swinney, eds. "Preparing Your Exhibits: Methods, Materials and Bibliography," *History News,* 24:9 (October 1969), Technical Leaflet no. 4.

Burns, William A. "Museum Exhibition: Do It Yourself or Commercial?" *Curator,* XII:3 (September 1969), pp. 160-167.

Burns, William A. "The Picture or the Frame?" *Environment Southwest,* May 1971. ♦ Reprinted in *The Museologist,* 120 (September 1971), pp. 6-11. Discusses the pros and cons of commercial exhibition firms versus permanent exhibition staff.

Calver, Homer N. "The Exhibit Medium," *American Journal of Public Health,* 29:4 (April 1939), pp. 341-346. ♦ Covers guidelines for effective exhibit techniques with an emphasis on various devices, such as label lettering, which engage visitor attention; how they work, the advantages and disadvantages of each device, and the psychological justification for their implementation.

Coleman, Laurence Vail. "Curatorial Work." In *Manual for Small Museums* (New York: G. P. Putnam's Sons, 1927), pp. 121-240.

Detroit Historical Museum. *Manual of Exhibit Properties.* Detroit: Detroit Historical Museum, 1956. 84 pp., illus.

"The Exhibit Room and its Equipment." In *Field Manual for Museums* (Ann Arbor, Mich.: Finch Press, 1974), pp. 4-58.

Faier, Samuel B. *Art of Display.* New York: M.S.R. Publications, 1948. 48 pp., illus.

Gaba, Lester. *The Art of Window Display.* New York: The Studio Publications, Inc. in association with Thomas Y. Crowell Co., 1952. 142 pp., illus.

Gardner, James, and Caroline Heller. *Exhibition and Display.* New York: F. W. Dodge Corporation, 1960. 191 pp., illus.

Gilbertson, Henry Walter. *Educational Exhibits, How to Prepare Them and Use Them; A Manual for Extension Workers.* Washington, D.C.: U.S. Government Printing Office, 1951. 41 pp., illus.

Gill, Edmund D. "Search for New Ideas on Museum Exhibits," *Curator,* X:4 (December 1967), pp. 275-278.

Glicksman, Hal. "A Guide to Art Installations," *Museum News,* 50:6 (February 1972), pp. 22-27. ♦ Technical aspects of planning and installing art exhibits.

Green, Martin. "Trends in Display Techniques," *CMA Gazette,* 4:4-5 (August-November 1970), pp. 1-18.

Hayett, William. *Display and Exhibit Handbook.* New York: Reinhold Publishing Co., 1967. 111 pp., illus.

Henderson, Stuart M.K., and Helen Kapp. *Special Exhibitions.* Handbook for Museum Curators, F2. London: The Museums Association, 1959. 22 pp.

Herdeg, Walter. *Window Display: An International Survey of the Art of Window Display.* New York: Frederick A. Praeger, 1961. 282 pp., illus.

Hirsch, Richard. "Exhibits and Installations: An Outline Guide," *History News,* 19:7 (May 1964), Technical Leaflet no. 20.

Howell, Daniel B. "A Network System for the Planning, Designing, Construction, and Installation of Exhibits," *Curator,* XIV:2 (June 1971), pp. 100-108.

Kapp, Reginald O. *The Presentation of Technical Information; Based on Four Public Lectures Given at University College, London.* New York: Macmillan Co., 1948. 147 pp.

Kroll, Natasha. *Window Display.* New York: Studio Publications, 1954. 96 pp., illus., bibliog.

Leydenfrost, Robert J. *Window Display.* New York: Architectural Book Publishing Company, 1950. 207 pp., illus.

Long, Charles J. *Museum Worker's Notebook.* New edition. San Antonio: The Author, 1970. various paging, illus., supply sources, bibliog., looseleaf. ◆ Gives brief explanations of recommended methods and equipment and provides a list of suppliers and manufacturers.

Mayo, Robert B. "A Strategy for Exhibitions," *Museum News,* 49:7 (March 1971), pp. 30-33. ◆ How to build exhibits on a low budget, get volunteer help, donated services and materials.

Mayor, A. Hyatt. "How to Bake an Exhibition," *The Museologist,* 93 (December 1964), pp. 7-12.

Miller, Ralph R. "Museum Installation," *The Museologist,* 95 (June 1965), pp. 4-10.

"Modern Trends of Display in Archaeological Museums," *Museum,* VI:1 (1953), entire issue.

"Museum Exhibition Techniques," *Midwest Museums Conference Quarterly,* 14:3 (July 1954), entire issue.

"Museum Exhibits." In *Field Manual for Museums* (Ann Arbor, Mich.: Finch Press, 1974), pp. 59-93.

Neal, Arminta. *Exhibits for the Small Museum; A Handbook.* With an Introductory Essay by H. J. Swinney. Nashville, Tenn.: American Association for State and Local History, 1976. 169 pp., photos, diagrams, appendices. ◆ This how-to-do-it manual discusses case exhibit design and installation, lighting, labels, mannikins, scale models, and adaptation of old buildings for exhibit purposes. Since this very useful publication is a continuation and expansion of *Help! For the Small Museum* by the same author, it has been included although published after the closing date for compilation.

Neal, Arminta. *Help! For the Small Museum; A Handbook of Exhibit Ideas and Methods.* Boulder, Colo.: Pruett Publishing, 1969. 200 pp., photos, drawings, diagrams, sources of supply, bibliog. ◆ Covers general principles, planning, design of exhibits, labels, color and light, case exhibits, construction notes, tools, materials.

Nelson, George, ed. *Display.* New York: Whitney Publishers, 1953. 190 pp., illus.

Osborn, Alan J. *Development of an Archaeological Museum Display.* Museum Briefs no. 2. Columbia, Mo.: Museum of Anthropology, University of Missouri, 1970. 10 pp., illus.

Pick, Beverley. *Display Presentation; Exhibitions, Window and Outdoor Displays.* London: C. Lockwood and Son., Ltd., 1957. 144 pp., illus.

Poole, H. H. *Fundamentals of Display Systems.* Washington, D.C.: Spartan Books, 1966. 403 pp., illus., maps, bibliog.

Porter, Daniel R. "Giving Your Museum a New Look," *History News,* 15:5 (March 1960), pp. 62-64.

Richman, Irwin. "Industrial and Organizational Sponsorship of Museum Exhibits," *History News,* 25:4 (April 1970), Technical Leaflet no. 54.

Roehr, Meta. "Corporate Exhibits in Museums," *Museum News,* 42:6 (February 1964), pp. 36-38. ◆ Discusses how a museum can best work with local and national firms in an exhibition program.

Rowe, Frank A. *Display Fundamentals: A Basic Display Manual.* Cincinnati, Ohio: Signs of the Times Publishing Co., 1965. 149 pp., illus.

Sweeney, James Johnson. "Some Ideas on Exhibition Installation," *Curator,* II:2 (1959), pp. 151-156.

Talmadge, R. H. *Point of Sale Display.* New York: The Studio Publications, 1958. 96 pp., illus., bibliog.

Warren, Jefferson T. *Exhibit Methods.* New York: Sterling Publishing Co., 1972. 80 pp., illus., appendices, index. ◆ Gives basic information on how to produce a small volunteer exhibit.

Weiss, Robert S., and Serge Boutourline, Jr. *Fairs, Pavilions, Exhibits, and Their Audiences.* Waltham, Mass.: The Author, 1962. 197 pp., illus. ◆ This study involved monitoring traffic flow throughout the fair as well as within pavilions. Considers the problem of lines and congestion, effects of exhibit techniques on the audience and the teaching potential of exhibits.

Welsh, Peter C. "Exhibit Planning: Ordering Your Artifacts Interpretively," *History News,* 29:4 (April 1974), Technical Leaflet no. 73.

Wetzel, Joseph. "Three Steps to Exhibit Success," *Museum News,* 50:6 (February 1972), pp. 20-21. ◆ A professional designer discusses how to ensure the success of your next exhibit.

Special Exhibit Problems

CASE EXHIBITS

Bloch, Milton J. "A Case of Boredom," *Museum News,* 47:9 (May 1969), pp. 21-24. ◆ Basic considerations in case exhibit design.

Bowditch, George. "Preparing Exhibits: Case and Prop Design," *History News,* 26:6 (June 1971), Technical Leaflet no. 12.

Bowditch, George. "Preparing Your Exhibits: Case Arrangement and Design," *History News,* 26:2 (February 1971), Technical Leaflet no. 56.

Neal, Arminta. *Designing an Exhibit Case: The Mock–Up.* Nashville, Tenn.: American Association for State and Local History, 1976. 15 minute cassette tape, slide carousel, supplementary material. Rental or purchase. ◆ An exhibit case is designed as a mock-up using scale model case furniture and labeling. Revision of *Exhibit Case Design* (1973).

Neal, Arminta. *Gallery and Case Design.* Nashville, Tenn.: American Association for State and Local History, 1973. 20 minute cassette tape, slide carousel, supplementary material. Rental or purchase. ◆ Describes the basic procedures in building a new exhibit, from writing the outline to traffic pattern concerns and final case construction.

Neal, Arminta. "Gallery and Case Exhibit Design," *Curator,* VI:1 (1963), pp. 77-95.

Neal, Arminta. "Gallery and Case Exhibit Design," *History News,* 24:8 (August 1969), Technical Leaflet no. 52.

Riviere, Georges H., and Herman F. E. Visser. "Museum Showcases," *Museum,* XIII:1 (1960), pp. 1-23.

TEMPORARY AND TRAVELLING EXHIBITS

Brayton, Frances. "School Loan Exhibits for the Local Historical Society," *History News,* 26:8 (August 1971), Technical Leaflet no. 16.

Butler, Patricia M. *Temporary Exhibitions.* Museums Association Information Sheet. London: The Museums Association, 1970. 4 pp. ◆ Includes planning, installation, opening, and the exhibition in progress.

Carmel, James. H. *Exhibition Techniques— Travelling and Temporary.* New York: Reinhold Publishing Corporation, 1962. 216 pp., illus., bibliog.

Grobman, Arnold B. "Museum Extension Through Travelling Museums," *Curator,* I:4 (Autumn 1958), pp. 82-88.

Lawless, Benjamin. "Museum Installations of a Semi-Permanent Nature," *Curator,* I:1 (January 1958), pp. 81-90.

Osborn, Elodie C. *Manual of Travelling Exhibitions.* Museums and Monuments—5. Paris: UNESCO, 1953. 111 pp., illus., bibliog.

Pond, Gordon G. *Science Materials: Preparation and Exhibition for the Classroom.* Rev. ed. Dubuque, Iowa: Wm. C. Brown Co., 1964. 148 pp., illus., index. ◆ Directed toward secondary school use, but ideas are adaptable, particularly to small museums.

Shosteck, Robert. "Travelling Facsimile Exhibits," *History News,* 29:1 (January 1974), Technical Leaflet no. 70.

United Nations Educational, Scientific, and Cultural Organization. *Temporary and Travelling Exhibitions.* Museums and Monuments—10. Paris: UNESCO, 1963. 123 pp., illus., bibliog., appendices.

Versteeg, Harvey. "Fabricating Bubble Top Cases for Portable Exhibits," *History News,*

29:10 (October 1974), Technical Leaflet no. 79.

Wakefield, Hugh, and Gabriel White. *Circulating Exhibitions.* Handbook for Museum Curators, F1. London: The Museums Association, 1959. 23 pp.

Webster, Donald B., Jr. "A Different Approach to Circulating School Exhibits," *Curator,* VIII:3 (1965), pp. 256-263.

Witteborg, Lothar P., and Henry Gardiner. "A New Temporary Exhibit System," *Curator,* IV:2 (1961), pp. 175-180.

NOTES

Smithsonian Institution Traveling Exhibition Service (SITES), Smithsonian Institution, Washington, D.C. 20560. Provides exhibits as a public service to educational, scientific, cultural and commercial institutions. Exhibits are available in paintings and sculpture, prints and drawings, architecture, decorative arts and design, history, children's art and toys, natural history, photography, reproductions and science and technology.

COSTUMES AND MANNIKINS

Askew, Richard B. M. "The Display and Preservation of Historic Costume Pieces for the Smaller Museum," *Midwest Museums Conference Quarterly,* 28:1 (Winter 1967-68), pp. 12-15.

Briggs, Rose T. "Displaying Your Costumes: Some Effective Techniques," rev. ed., *History News,* 27:11 (November 1972), Technical Leaflet no. 33.

Cofer, Janet. *Manikins for the Small Museum.* Museum Briefs no. 3. Columbia, Mo.: Museum of Anthropology, University of Missouri, 1970. 20 pp., illus., bibliog.

Collard, Eileen. *Patterns of Fashions of the 1870's.* Burlington, Ontario: Joseph Brant Museum, 1971. 22 pp., illus.

Coutchie, Mariann. *Jewelry on Display.* Cincinnati, Ohio: Signs of the Times Publishing Co., 1972. 83 pp., illus. ◆ Oriented toward the commercial display of jewelry but has many useful ideas that can be adapted for museum use.

Freeman, Joan, and H. Charles Fritzemeier. "Preparing Your Exhibits: Figures for Miniature Dioramas," *History News,* 27:7 (July 1972), Technical Leaflet no. 20.

Halvorson, Elmer. "Constructing Life-Size Figures for the Historical Museum," *History News,* 28:6 (June 1973), Technical Leaflet no. 64.

"How Betty Odle Made the Wayanas," *The Museologist,* 115 (June 1970), pp. 22-23. ◆ Describes transformation of female mannequins into Wayana Indians.

OTHER PROBLEMS

Behrnd, Henry. "From Both Sides Now," *Museum News,* 51:5 (January 1973), pp. 29-30. ◆ Describes how to display coins in clear plastic.

Clarke, R. Rainbird. "The Display of Archaeological Material," *Museums Journal,* 53:12 (March 1954), pp. 310-319.

Gold, Peter. "Music Under Glass: New Approaches to the Exhibition of Sound Producing Instruments," *Curator,* XIV:3 (September 1971), pp. 159-174.

Jones, William K. "The Exhibit of Documents: Preparation, Matting and Display Techniques," *History News,* 29:6 (June 1974), Technical Leaflet no. 75.

Leisinger, Albert H., Jr. "The Exhibit of Documents," *The American Archivist,* 26:1 (January 1963), pp. 75-86.

Little, Nina Fletcher. "Historic Houses: An Approach to Furnishing," *History News,* 25:2 (February 1970), Technical Leaflet no. 17.

National Trust for Historic Preservation. *How to Organize a Needlework Show.* Washington, D.C.: The Trust, 1971. 8 pp., illus., bibliog. ◆ Gives tips on materials, record-keeping, display, insurance, judges, etc.

Quirk, Marie S. "Historical Dioramas at Holyoke Museum: Space-Saving Displays for Small Museums with Limited Budgets," *Curator,* XII:2 (June 1969), pp. 125-133.

Special Exhibit Techniques

LIGHTING

Bloch, Milton. "Lighting," *Museum News,* 47:5 (January 1969), pp. 20-29.

Brommelle, N. S., and J. B. Harris. "Museum Lighting, Part I," *Museums Journal,* 61:3 (December 1961), pp. 169-177.

Brommelle, N. S., and J. B. Harris. "Museum Lighting, Part 2—Artificial Lighting and Museums Display," *Museums Journal,* 61:4 (March 1962), pp. 259-267.

Brommelle, N. S., and J. B. Harris. "Museum Lighting, Part 3—Aspects of the Effect of Light on Deterioration," *Museums Journal,* 62:1 (June 1962), pp. 337-346.

Brommelle, N. S., and J. B. Harris. "Museum Lighting, Part 4—Viewing the Object," *Museums Journal,* 62:3 (December 1962), pp. 178-186.

Crawford, B. H. "Just Perceptible Colour Differences in Relation to Level of Illumination," *Studies in Conservation,* 18:4 (November 1973), pp. 159-166.

Harris, J. B. "Museum Lighting," *Museums Journal,* 63:1 & 2 (June-September 1963), pp. 36-42.

Hatt, Robert T. "Seven Lighting Problems: Seven Solutions," *Curator,* III:4 (1960), pp. 361-370.

Howard, Richard F. "Museum Lighting," *Museum News,* 40:7 (March 1962), pp. 22-27.

Illuminating Engineering Society. *IES Lighting Handbook: The Standard Lighting Guide.* 5th ed. New York: Illuminating Engineering Society, 1972. various paging, illus., bibliog. ♦ Includes a section on libraries, museums and art galleries.

Kelly, Richard. "Museum Lighting, Part III," *Museum News,* 37:3 (May 1959), pp. 16-19.

Lusk, Carroll B. "Museum Lighting," *Museum News,* 49:3 (November 1970), pp. 20-22.

Lusk, Carroll B. "Museum Lighting II," *Museum News,* 49:4 (December 1970), pp. 25-29.

Lusk, Carroll B. "Museum Lighting III," *Museum News,* 49:6 (February 1971), pp. 18-22.

McCandless, Stanley. "Museum Lighting, Part I," *Museum News,* 37:1 (March 1959), pp. 8-11.

McCandless, Stanley. "Museum Lighting, Part II," *Museum News,* 37:2 (April 1959), pp. 8-11.

PERIODICALS

International Lighting Review. 1950, quarterly, subscription. Foundation "Prometheus", NZ Voorburgwal 271-273, Amsterdam C, Netherlands.

LABELS

Bloch, Milton. "Labels, Legends and Legibility," *Museum News,* 47:3 (November 1968), pp. 13-17.

Boley, Bill. *Bill Boley Basiks of Lettering.* Cincinnati, Ohio: Signs of the Times Publishing Co., 1952. 192 pp., illus. ♦ Illustrates how each lettering stroke is made, how to hold the lettering brush and provides advice on how to master the art of brush lettering.

Butkowski, Patricia. *A Look You'll Like in Labels.* Detroit, Mich.: Detroit Historical Society, 1960. 36 pp., illus.

Cavanagh, J. S. *Lettering and Alphabets.* New York: Dover Publications, 1955. 121 pp., illus. ♦ Deals with built-up lettering and a variety of useful faces. Originally published in 1946 under the title *Lettering.*

Christensen, Erwin O. "Labels for Masterpieces," *Museum News,* 43:9 (May 1965), pp. 29-31.

Conaway, Mary Ellen. "Exhibit Labeling: Another Alternative," *Curator,* XV:2 (June 1972), pp. 161-166.

Conway, Wallace X. "Increasing the Life of Graphic Materials," *Museum News,* 50:6 (February 1972), pp. 28-31. ♦ Describes the fiberglass embedment process which offers minimum maintenance and increased longevity for exhibits.

Cooper, Margaret. "How to Cut a Label," *Curator,* XI:4 (1968), pp. 290-291.

Cordingly, David. *Methods of Lettering for Museums.* Museums Association Information Sheet no. 15. London: Museums Association, 1972. 5 pp.

Dair, Carl. *Design With Type.* Toronto: University of Toronto Press, 1967. 128 pp., illus.

Denyer, Edward F. "Silk Screen Printing and Museum Exhibits," *Curator,* VII:3 (1964), pp. 185-195.

Flesch, Rudolf. *The Art of Readable Writing.* New York: Macmillan and Co., 1962. 255 pp., illus., bibliog. footnotes.

Garland, Ken. *Graphics Handbook.* New York: Reinhold Publishing Corporation, 1966. 96 pp., illus., tables, diagrams, bibliog.

Johnston, Edward. *Writing and Illuminating and Lettering.* Rev. ed. 1944. Reprint. New York: Pitman Publishing Corporation, 1962, 439 pp., illus., facsimile.

Longyear, William. *Type and Lettering.* 4th ed., rev. and enl. New York: Watson-Guptill Publications, Inc., 1966. 175 pp., illus.

Neal, Arminta. "Legible Labels: Hand-Lettering," rev. ed., *History News,* 26:7 (July 1971), Technical Leaflet no. 22.

Neal, Arminta. *Legible Labels: Three Dimensional Letters.* Rev. ed. Technical Leaflet no. 23. Nashville, Tenn.: American Association for State and Local History, 1971. 8 pp., illus.

North, F. J. *Museum Labels.* London: The Museums Association, 1957. 42 pp., illus., bibliog.

Oliphant, Robert; James Claus; and Karen Claus. *Psychological Considerations of Lettering for Identification.* Cincinnati, Ohio: Signs of the Times Publishing Co., 1971. 47 pp., illus. ♦ Basic examination of lettering with suggestions as to proper spacing; design and other considerations in effective lettering.

Spencer, Herbert. *The Visible Word: Problems of Legibility.* New York: Visual Communications Books, Hastings House, 1968. 107 pp., illus., glossary, bibliog. ♦ An examination of alphabet form, word spacing, line spacing, etc., in effectiveness and legibility.

Weiner, George. "Why Johnny Can't Read Labels," *Curator,* VI:2 (1963), pp. 143-156. ♦ Detailed description of all aspects of labeling including length, content, size of lettering, type of lettering, and positioning; discusses the important effects these aspects have on the museum visitor.

Williams, Luther A. "Labels: Writing, Design, and Preparation," *Curator,* III:1 (1960), pp. 26-42.

Wilson, C. P. "Museum Labels," *CMA Gazette,* 4:4-5 (August-November 1970), pp. 32-36.

Wilson, Don, and Dennis Medina. "Exhibit Labels: A Consideration of Content," *History News,* 27:4 (April 1972), Technical Leaflet no. 60.

NOTES

Transfer lettering is ideal for the preparation of camera-ready art for offset reproduction, for applying names to certificates, for labels and other uses. It is available from Prestype, Inc., Gotham Industrial Park, 194 Veterans Blvd., Carlstadt, New Jersey 07072; Letraset U.S.A., Inc., 2379 Charleston Road, Mountain View, California 94040.

USE OF COLOR

Birren, Faber. *Color for Interiors, Historical and Modern: An Essential Reference Work Covering the Major Period Styles of History and Including Modern Pallets for the Authentic Decoration of Homes, Institutions, and Commercial Interiors.* New York: Whitney Library of Design, 1963. 210 pp., illus.

Cheskin, Louis. *Colors: What They Can Do For You.* New York: Liveright Publishing Corp., 1951. 214 pp., illus.

Danger, Eric P. *How to Use Color to Sell.* Boston: Cahners Publishing Co., Inc., 1969. 224 pp., illus., bibliog., index, appendices. ♦ Written for marketing and advertisers but has useful advice that can be adapted for museum galleries and exhibits.

Longyear, William L. *How to Use Color in Advertising Design, Illustration and Painting.* New York: Pitman Publishing Co., 1949. 40 pp., illus.

Luckiesh, Matthew. *Color and Colors.* New York: D. Van Nostrand Co., Inc., 1938. 206 pp.

MANUAL ARTS

Better Homes and Gardens Handymans Book. Rev. ed. Des Moines: Meredith Publishing Co., 1970. 400 pp., illus.

Gladstone, Bernard. *Hints and Tips for the Handyman.* Rev. ed. New York: Pitman Publishing Co., 1960. 125 pp., illus.

Reader's Digest Complete Do-It-Yourself Manual. Pleasantville, N.Y.: Reader's Digest Association, 1973. 600 pp., photos, drawings, diagrams, plans, index. ♦ With this book a one-person staff can do everything from elementary plumbing repairs to building exhibits.

Stanley Works, New Britain, Connecticut. Stanley Tools Division. *How to Work With Tools* *and Wood.* Edited by Robert Campbell and N. H. Mager. New York: Pocket Books, 1965. 488 pp., illus.

OTHER TECHNIQUES

Belcher, M. *Wall Coverings.* Museums Association Information Sheet no. 13. London: Museums Association, 1972. 11 pp. ◆ Provides curators with information on the diversity of materials which are available, their suitability for various uses within the museum, and where they can be obtained. Includes information on wallpapers, cork, fabrics, hardfacings, laminates and boards, metals, paints and sprays, veneers, photomurals and paneling.

Belcher, M.; K. Heathcote; and G. Stansfield. *Silk Screen Printing.* Museums Association Information Sheet no. 16. London: Museums Association, 1973. 4 pp.

Biegeleisen, Jacob I. *The Complete Book of Silk Screen Printing Production.* New York: Dover Publication, 1963. 253 pp., illus., bibliog.

Bowditch, George. "Constructing Modular Furniture," *History News,* 28:12 (December 1973), Technical Leaflet no. 69.

Bowditch, George. "Ideas: Preparing the Groundwork for Exhibits Where Earth Surfaces are Needed," *History News,* 25:6 (June 1970), pp. 132-133.

Carmel, James H. "Exhibit Framework and Structural Framing Systems," *Curator,* V:3 (1962), pp. 265-302.

Chedister, Ron. "Museum Audio-Visuals, Or, Play it Again Sam," *Museum News,* 50:6 (February 1972), pp. 32-35. ◆ Discusses various kinds of audio-visual equipment which can be used in exhibits.

Davis, Gordon, and Wesley Hurt. "Designs of Modular Exhibit Units," *Curator,* XVI:2 (June 1973), pp. 158-168.

Horn, George. *Visual Communication: Bulletin Boards, Exhibits, Visual Aids.* Worcester, Mass.: Davis Publishing Co., 1973. 95 pp., illus.

Howard, James H. *Electronic Information Displays for Management.* 1st ed. Detroit: American Data Processing, 1966. 110 pp., illus., bibliog.

Jones, William K. "Preparing Exhibits: The Use of Plexiglas," *History News,* 24:2 (February 1969), Technical Leaflet no. 49.

Jones, William K., and Dennis Medina. *Wet and Dry Mounting Photographs.* Nashville, Tenn.: American Association for State and Local History, 1975. 15 minute tape cassette, slide carousel, supplementary material. Rental or purchase. ◆ Explains step by step procedure for the wet mounting of oversize photographs for use in exhibits. Instructions are also given for using a dry mount press.

Jones, William K., and Dennis Medina. *Working with Plexiglas.* Nashville, Tenn.: American Association for State and Local History, 1975. 20 minute tape cassette, slide carousel, supplementary material. Rental or purchase. ◆ Shows the construction of a display box and bracket made of plastic acrylic sheeting (commonly known as plexiglas). Demonstrations of cutting, joining, and bending with heat and a general discussion of plexiglas's potential as a display material are included.

Kane, Jean Duval. "Setting Up a Silk-Screening Facility: Guidelines for the Small Museum," *History News,* 28:11 (November 1973), Technical Leaflet no. 68.

Kelly, Frank S. "Setting the STAGE for Exhibits," *Museum News,* 52:1 (September 1973), pp. 42-45. ◆ Describes STORESTAGE, an exhibit system designed for department stores but which can be adapted easily for museum use. The author suggests that the systems concept may set new standards for the relationship between museum buildings and their contents.

Kissiloff, William. "How to Use Mixed Media in Exhibits," *Curator,* XII:2 (June 1969), pp. 83-95.

Kosloff, Albert. *Ceramic Screen Printing.* Cincinnati, Ohio: Signs of the Times Publishing Co., 1962. 97 pp., illus. ◆ Describes in detail the various aspects of ceramic colors, firing, ceramic decals, methods and printing.

Kosloff, Albert. *Photographic Screen Process Printing.* 3rd ed. Cincinnati, Ohio: Signs of the Times Publishing Co., 1972. 304 pp., illus.

◆ Covers all phases of photoscreen reproduction.

Kosloff, Albert. *Screen Process Printing.* 3rd ed. Cincinnati, Ohio: Signs of the Times Publishing Co., 1964. 336 pp., illus. ◆ A basic book on screen printing techniques.

Kosloff, Albert. *Textile Screen Printing.* Cincinnati, Ohio: Signs of the Times Publishing Co., 1966. 131 pp., illus.

Libin, Laurence. "Two Sense Worth," *Museum News,* 52:5 (January-February 1974), pp. 50-52. ◆ Describes an audio-assisted gallery in which musical instruments speak for themselves.

Neal, Arminta. "New Uses for Styrofoam Plastic in Museum Display," *Curator,* V:2 (1962), pp. 128-136.

Randall, Reino, and Edward C. Haines. *Bulletin Boards and Display.* Worcester, Mass.: Davis Publications, Inc., 1961. 64 pp., illus.

Riefstahl, Rudolph M. "Museum Photography," *Museum News,* 44:2 (October 1965), pp. 21-23.

Rovetti, Paul F. "Supermarketing Your Exhibit," *Museum News,* 51:4 (December 1972), pp. 35-36. ◆ Describes how to package an exhibit in cardboard boxes.

Ruskin, B. F. "Treatment of Museum Walls," *Museum News,* 43:3 (November 1964), pp. 31-33.

Exhibits and Conservation

Brommelle, Norman S. "Lighting, Air-Conditioning, Exhibition, Storage, Handling, and Packing." In *The Conservation of Cultural Property with Special Reference to Tropical Conditions* (Paris: UNESCO, 1968), pp. 291-303.

Cursiter, Stanley. "Control of Air in Cases and Frames," *Technical Studies in the Field of the Fine Arts,* V:2 (October 1936), pp. 109-116.

Harris, J. B. "Practical Aspects of Lighting as Related to Conservation." In *Contributions to the London Conference on Museum Climatology* (London: International Institute for Conservation, 1968), pp. 133-138.

Harrison, Laurence S. "Evaluation of Spectral Radiation Hazards in Window-lighted Galleries." In *Recent Advances in Conservation* (London: Butterworths, 1963), pp. 1-6.

Illuminating Engineering Society, London. *Lighting of Art Galleries and Museums.* Illuminating Engineering Society Technical Report 14. London: The Society, 1970. 33 pp., illus.

Keck, Caroline K. "On Conservation: Converting Fluorescent Lighting in Museum Cases," *Museum News,* 50:7 (March 1972), p. 13.

Keck, Caroline K. *Safeguarding Your Collection in Travel.* Nashville, Tenn.: American Association for State and Local History, 1970. 78 pp., illus. ◆ Provides instructions for pre-shipment inspection, packing, transporting and insurance. Illustrations show procedures for making photographic records and solving specific packing problems.

Organ, R. M. "Humidification of Galleries for a Temporary Exhibition." In *Contributions to the London Conference on Museum Climatology* (London: International Institute for Conservation, 1968), pp. 1-13.

Padfield, Tim. "The Control of Relative Humidity and Air Pollution in Showcases and Picture Frames," *Studies in Conservation,* 11:1 (February 1966), pp. 8-30.

Padfield, Tim. "Design of Museum Showcases." In *Contributions to the London Conference on Museum Climatology* (London: International Institute for Conservation, 1968), pp. 119-126.

Riefstahl, Rudolph M. "Museum Installation: Display or Destruction," *Midwest Museums Conference Quarterly,* 26:3 (Summer 1966), pp. 4-6.

Sekino, Masaru, and Kenzo Toishi. "The Fine Arts Museum at Expo '70, Osaka: Conservation Techniques," *Museum,* XXIV:1 (1972), pp. 67-88. ◆ Discusses security, air conditioning, heating, lighting, temperature and humidity, and monitoring systems.

Stolow, Nathan. "Fundamental Case Design for Humidity Sensitive Collections," *Museum News,* 44:6 (February 1966), Technical Supplement no. 11.

U.S. National Bureau of Standards. *Protec-*

tive Display Lighting of Historical Documents: A Report to the Library of Congress. Washington, D.C.: U.S. Government Printing Office, 1953. 8 pp., illus.

Exhibit Descriptions

Anderson, Duane C. "Creative Teaching, Temporary Exhibits, and Vitality for the Small Museum," *Curator,* XII:3 (September 1969), pp. 180-183. ◆ Describes a long-term temporary exhibition program at the Sanford Museum in Cherokee, Iowa.

Bloch, Linda. "The Red Box: An Improvised Suitcase Exhibit," *Museum News,* 47:7 (March 1969), pp. 29-31. ◆ Describes a traveling exhibit, circulated to schools from the Little Rock Museum of Science and Natural History, intended to stimulate curiosity about natural objects.

Borhegyi, Stephan F. de, and Patricia Hampton. "A Primitive Art Exhibit by University Students," *Curator,* IV:1 (1961), pp. 7-14.

Dailey, Daniel, and Roger Mandle. "Welcome to the Museum," *Museum News,* 52:5 (January-February 1974), pp. 45-49.

Devenish, David C. "Methods and Problems of Archaeological Display in British Provincial Museums," *Curator,* IX:2 (1966), pp. 156-165.

Dodson, O. H. "Surprise Assistance for a Small Museum," *Curator,* XIII:3 (September 1970), pp. 216-225.

Kane, Lucile. "The Exhibition of Manuscripts at the Minnesota Historical Society," *The American Archivist,* 15:1 (January 1952), pp. 39-45.

Munro, Alan R. "The Yellow Submarine," *Museum News,* 46:6 (February 1968), pp. 20-23. ◆ Describes the mobile museum of the Children's Museum in Nashville, Tennessee.

Pinney, Janet. "The 'Please Touch' Exhibit," *Curator,* II:4 (1959), pp. 339-347.

Robbins, Michael. "SAM [Student Art Mobile] Explains," *Museum News,* 47:8 (April 1969), pp. 19-21.

"Rolling Museum Takes Education to Isolated Northern Canadians," *History News,* 29:1 (January 1974), pp. 6-7.

Rovetti, Paul F. "3 Museums, 1 Exhibition," *Museum News,* 47:7 (March 1969), pp. 22-24. ◆ Describes a cooperative exhibit by the New Britain Museum of American Art, Lyman Allen Museum, and Mattatuck Museum.

Taylor, James B., et al. *Science on Display; A Study of the United States Science Exhibit, Seattle World's Fair, 1962.* Seattle: Institute for Sociological Research, University of Washington, 1963. 185 pp.

Thomas, W. Stephen. "A New Museum Orientation Theatre: An Experiment in Interpreting Exhibits at the Rochester Museum and Science Center," *The Museologist,* 122 (March 1972), pp. 18-20.

Wakefield, Hugh. "Travelling Exhibitions," *Museum,* XXIII:2 (1970-1971), pp. 146-149. ◆ Describes the travelling exhibition and collection of the National Museum Loan Service in Great Britain.

Welsh, Peter C. "Folk Art and the History Museum: The Van Alstyne Collection at the Smithsonian Institution," *Curator,* X:1 (March 1967), pp. 60-78.

White, Dana F. "Back Bay Boston: A Museum Experiment with Urban History," *Museum News,* 48:7 (March 1970), pp. 20-25.

Yenawine, Philip. "Extending the Met," *Museum News,* 48:10 (June 1970), pp. 30-32. ◆ Describes a portable exhibit series which brings quality reproductions to New York City schools.

Yervasi, Rocco. "The Exhibit: A Corporate Concept," *The Museologist,* 116 (September 1970), pp. 12-16. ◆ Describes Xerox Square Exhibit Center, Rochester, New York.

Exhibit Evaluation

Battison, Edwin A. "Exhibit Review: Technological Innovation and the Decorative Arts: Hagley Museum, March 29, 1973-January 1, 1974," *Technology and Culture,* 15:2 (April 1974), pp. 242-245.

Borhegyi, Stephan F. de. "Museum Exhibits, How to Plan and Evaluate Them," *Midwest Museums Conference Quarterly,* 23:2 (Spring 1963), pp. 4-8. ◆ Concise statement of the need for exhibit evaluation and the use of special test exhibits to measure visitor retention and participation.

Cameron, Duncan F. "Measuring Effectiveness: The Evaluator's Viewpoint," *Museum News*, 46:5 (January 1968), pp. 43-45. ◆ Covers many problems of exhibit evaluation such as design and instrumentation.

Cotter, John L. "Exhibit Review: Colonial Williamsburg," *Technology and Culture*, 11:3 (July 1970), pp. 417-427.

Davis, Robert C. "Exhibit Review: The Brass Age of Psychology," *Technology and Culture*, 11:4 (October 1970), pp. 604-612. ◆ Review of the Laboratory Instruments Exhibit of the Archives of the History of American Psychology, University of Akron, Ohio.

Ferguson, Eugene S. "Exhibit Review: Hall of Power Machinery, Museum of History and Technology, U.S. National Museum," *Technology and Culture*, 9:1 (January 1968), pp. 75-85.

Hilton, George W. "Exhibit Review: The Dossin Great Lakes Museum," *Technology and Culture*, 11:2 (April 1970), pp. 289-297. ◆ Reviews the Dossin Great Lakes Museum, Belle Isle, Detroit, Michigan.

Hippen, James C. "Exhibit Review: Industrial Textile Machinery: Five North American Museums," *Technology and Culture*, 10:4 (October 1969), pp. 570-586. ◆ The five museums are: Watkins Mill State Park, Lawson, Missouri; Upper Canada Village, Morrisburg, Ontario; Henry Ford Museum and Greenfield Village, Dearborn, Michigan; Old Slater Mill Museum, Pawtucket, Rhode Island; and Little Red Shop, Hopedale, Massachusetts.

Kimmel, Peter S., and Mark J. Maves. "Public Reaction to Museum Interiors," *Museum News*, 51:1 (September 1972), pp. 17-19. ◆ A team at the University of California at Berkeley completed research on art museum environments through user evaluation of lighting and wall and floor coverings.

Leavitt, Thomas W. "The Need for Critical Standards in History Museum Exhibits: A Case in Point," *Curator*, X:2 (June 1967), pp. 91-94.

Leavitt, Thomas W. "Toward a Standard of Excellence: The Nature and Purpose of Exhibit Reviews," *Technology and Culture*, 9:1 (January 1968), pp. 70-75.

Lewis, W. David. "Exhibit Review: Corning Museum of Glass," *Technology and Culture*, 10:1 (January 1969), pp. 68-83.

Nicol, Elizabeth H. *The Development of Validated Museum Exhibits*. Washington, D.C.: U.S. Department of Health, Education and Welfare, Office of Education, Bureau of Research, 1969. 114 pp. ◆ Available from ERIC Document Reproduction Service, Computer Microfilm International Corporation, P.O. Box 190, Arlington, Virginia 22210. ERIC # ED 035 038. Discusses the museum as a learning environment. Exhibit development is treated as an evolutionary process, drawing the museum visitor into the collaborative venture of testing and improving the exhibits.

Parr, Albert E. "Some Basic Problems of Visual Education by Means of Exhibits," *Curator*, V:1 (1963), pp. 36-44.

Parr, Albert E. "Temporary Exhibition Versus Education," *Curator*, V:4 (1962), pp. 369-370.

Parsons, Lee A. "Systematic Testing of Display Techniques for an Anthropological Exhibit," *Curator*, VIII:2 (1965), pp. 167-189.

Richman, Irwin. "Exhibit Review: Hopewell Village National Historic Site," *Technology and Culture*, 9:2 (April 1968), pp. 213-217. ◆ Reviews Hopewell Village National Historic Site, R.F.D. #1, Elverson, Pennsylvania.

Shettel, Harris H., et al. *Strategies for Determining Exhibit Effectiveness*. Washington, D.C.: U.S. Department of Health, Education and Welfare, Office of Education, Bureau of Research, 1968. 229 pp., charts, tables, graphs, appendices, bibliog. ◆ Available from ERIC Document Reproduction Service, Computer Microfilm International Corporation, P.O. Box 190, Arlington, Virginia 22210. ERIC # ED 026 718. This study was undertaken "to initiate the systematic development of research strategies that will make it possible to better evaluate the effectiveness of scientific and technical exhibits, particularly those designed to reach educational objectives."

Washburn, Wilcomb E. "The Dramatization of American Museums," *Curator*, VI:2 (1963), pp. 109-124.

Weiss, Robert S., and Serge Bouterline, Jr. "The Communication Value of Exhibits," *Museum News*, 47:3 (November 1963), pp.

23-27. ◆ Describes a survey conducted at the Boston Science Museum.

White, Dana F. "Exhibit Review: The Apocalyptic Vision of Paolo Soleri," *Technology and Culture,* 12:1 (January 1971), pp. 75-88. ◆ Review of "The Architectural Vision of Paolo Soleri" at the Corcoran Gallery of Art, February 20-April 5, 1970; at the Whitney Museum, July 17-September 20, 1970.

White, John H., Jr. "Exhibit Review: Baltimore and Ohio Transportation Museum," *Technology and Culture,* 11:1 (January 1970), pp. 70-84.

Witteborg, Lothar P. "Design Standards in Museum Exhibits," *Curator,* I:1 (January 1958), pp. 29-41.

Wright, Gilbert. "Some Criteria for Evaluating Displays in Museums," *Midwest Museums Conference Quarterly,* 18:3 (1958), pp. 62-70.

NOTES

Exhibit Reviews, *Technology and Culture.* Begun in 1968, the exhibit reviews serve as a forum for scholarly exposition, constructive criticism and debate.

7

Museums in the Media Age

In this age of media, when the "medium is the message," museum visitors, accustomed to more and increasingly sophisticated uses of audiovisuals in all areas of their lives, expect it also in the museum. Historical organization personnel must be prepared to meet this demand either by including such media in their programs or by justifying its exclusion. This chapter, Museums in the Media Age, deals with the fields of audiovisuals, instructional technology, and computers as they relate, or fail to relate, to the interpretive function of museums. A media program can range from a simple slide lecture, to an automated slide unit as part of an exhibit, to a full scale instructional media center. References in this chapter encompass the whole gamut of such programs. In addition, there are strong arguments against the use of audiovisual media in the museum context.

The first section, Media and Teaching, provides references on the use of audiovisuals in teaching and their effectiveness as teaching tools. As schools come to rely more and more heavily on audiovisuals, museums must adapt programs and materials to fill this need. To do this properly they must understand how such materials are used.

Museums and the Media deals with specific applications of the media in museum activities: audiovisuals in exhibits, computerized guide systems, television programs produced by museums, videotapes, slide shows, programmed instruction.

References in Media Techniques provide practical advice on virtually every aspect of producing audiovisuals: photography, filmmaking, photocopying, animation, sound recording, slide production, projectors (both slide and film), videotape, slide/tape productions, and television.

Administering Instructional Media Programs offers a few references to those museums which are involved in large-scale instructional media programs. They provide some practical advice on such matters as ordering, distribution, service systems, and physical facilities.

Sources of Audiovisual Materials and Equipment lists directories, guides, indexes, bibliographies, checklists, catalogs, periodicals and organizations which will be helpful to a museum in assembling a collection of audiovisual materials and/or equipment.

Media and Teaching

Bagdikian, Ben. *The Information Machines: Their Impact on Men and Media.* New York: Harper & Row, 1971. 359 pp., illus., bibliog. references. ◆ Examines computers, cable TV, communications satellites, and the future development of video as an information transmission medium.

Bitzer, Donald L.; E. R. Lyman; and J. A. Easby, Jr. "The Uses of PLATO: A Computer Controlled Teaching System," *Audiovisual Instruction,* 11:1 (January 1966), pp. 16-21.

The Center for Understanding Media. *Doing the Media: A Portfolio of Activities and Resources.* New York: The Center, 1972. 221 pp., illus., bibliog.

Dale, Edgar. *Audiovisual Methods in Teaching.* 3rd ed. New York: Dryden Press, 1969. 719 pp., illus., bibliog., sources of teaching materials. ◆ Organized into three parts: theory and practice of audiovisual teaching; media and materials of audiovisual teaching; and systems and technology in teaching.

Dwyer, Francis M. *A Guide for Improving Visualized Instruction.* State College, Pa.: Pennsylvania State College, 1972. 138 pp., illus., bibliog. references.

Edling, Jack V. *A Basic Reference Shelf on Instructional Media Research.* Washington, D.C.: U.S. Office of Education, 1957. 9 pp. ◆ Reproduced from microfilm copy by ERIC Clearinghouse on Educational Media and Technology, 1968.

ERIC Clearinghouse on Media and Technology. *Museums and Media: A Status Report,* prepared by Richard Grove; and *Museums and Media: A Basic Reference Shelf,* by Philip Ritterbush. Stanford, Calif.: ERIC Clearinghouse on Educational Media and Technology at the Institute for Communication Research, Stanford University, 1970. 15 pp. ◆ Based on a paper prepared for the President's Commission on Instructional Technology in 1968. Bibliography lists books, papers, periodicals and reports to help show the important role museums play in elementary and secondary education.

Erickson, Carlton W. H., and David H. Curl. *Fundamentals of Teaching with Audiovisual Technology.* 2nd ed. New York: The Macmillan Co., 1972. 381 pp., illus., bibliog. ◆ Discusses the need for audiovisual technology with emphasis on newer instructional media. Includes numerous case studies and unique characteristics of each medium. Tells how to prepare simple materials and operate equipment.

Freedman, Florence B., and Esther L. Berg. *Classroom Teacher's Guide to Audio-Visual Materials.* New and enl. ed. Philadelphia: Chilton Books Educational Division, 1967. 279 pp., illus. ◆ Includes lesson plans and practical suggestions in the use of audiovisual materials.

Frye, Roy A. *Graphic Tools for Teachers.* 3rd ed. Austin, Tex.: E and I Printing Co., 1965. 105 pp., illus., bibliog.

Gagné, Robert Mills. *Media and the Learning Process.* Stanford, Calif.: ERIC Clearinghouse on Media and Technology, Stanford University, 1968. 14 pp. ◆ Available from ERIC Document Reproduction Service, Computer Microfilm International Corporation Inc., P.O. Box 190, Arlington, Virginia 22210.

Gagné, Robert M., and George L. Gropper, et al. *Studies in Film Instruction.* Pittsburgh: American Institutes for Research, 1965. various paging, illus., bibliog.

Gerlach, Vernon S., and Donald P. Ely. *Teaching and Media: A Systematic Approach.* Englewood Cliffs, N.J.: Prentice-Hall, Inc., 1971. 392 pp., illus., bibliog.

Kinder, James. *Using Audio-Visual Materials in Education.* New York: American Book Co., 1965. 199 pp., illus., bibliog.

Kuhns, William. *Exploring Television: An Inquiry/Discovery Program.* Chicago: Loyola University Press, 1971. 240 pp., illus., bibliog. ◆ Aimed at helping people to understand, analyze, criticize, evaluate and judge the experiences they have had in front of the TV set. 5th-6th grade level. Teachers' Guide is available which provides background information, guidelines on the text, resource listings and some educational philosophizing.

Lemler, Fred. "The Teacher and the Media," *Audiovisual Instruction,* 15:5 (May 1970), pp. 47-49. ◆ Guidelines for teachers which may be helpful to museum educators.

Lewis, Richard B. *The Effective Use of Media in Innovative Schools.* Stanford, Calif.: ERIC Clearinghouse on Information Resources, 1973. 15 pp., bibliog. ◆ Abstracts of ERIC documents on the effective use of media in innovative schools: elementary and secondary, higher education, adult education, developing countries. Available from ERIC Document Reproduction Service, Computer Microfilm International Corporation, Inc., P.O. Box 190, Arlington, Virginia 22210.

Litchtenberg, Mitchell P., and Edwin Fenton. "Using AV Materials Inductively in the Social Studies," *Audiovisual Instruction,* 11:5 (May 1966), p. 330.

Margulies, Stuart, and Lewis D. Eigen. *Applied Programmed Instruction.* New York: John Wiley, 1962. 387 pp., illus.

Morlan, John E. *Preparation of Inexpensive Teaching Materials.* 2nd ed. New York: Chandler Publishing Co., 1973. 180 pp., illus., bibliog., materials sources.

Tickton, Sidney G., comp. *To Improve Learning; An Evaluation of Instruction Technology.* New York: R. R. Bowker Co., 1970. 1 vol.

Willis, Edgar E. *Writing Television and Radio Programs.* New York: Holt, Rinehart and Winston, Inc., 1967. 372 pp., illus., bibliog.

PERIODICALS

Educational Technology. 1961, monthly, subscription. Educational Technology Publications, Inc., 140 Sylvan Avenue, Englewood Cliffs, N.J. 07632.

Museums and the Media

Adler, Billy, and John Margolies. "The Television Environment," *Museum News,* 52:5 (January-February 1974), pp. 58-59. ◆ Two West Coast artists have developed an interactive TV exhibit designed to let viewers watch this ephemeral medium in a museum context.

Auer, James M. "Menasha Historical Society Produces a Motion Picture," *History News,* 17:9 (July 1962), pp. 134-136.

Bitzer, Donald L. "The Computer: A Flexible Guide to Art Museums." In *Computers and their Potential Applications in Museums* (New York: Arno Press, 1968), pp. 349-357.

Bluem, A. William. *Documentary in American Television: Form, Function and Method.* New York: Hastings House, 1965. 311 pp., illus., bibliog.

Chedister, Ron. "Museum Audio-Visuals, Or, Play it Again Sam," *Museum News,* 50:6 (February 1972), pp. 32-35. ◆ Discusses various kinds of audio-visual equipment which can be used in exhibits (sound systems, movies, slide projectors).

Cheney, Jane M. B. "Television . . . Voracious? Veracious? A Museum's Experience in Television Production," *The Museologist,* 116 (September 1970), pp. 23-25. ◆ Describes television efforts of the Hartford Children's Museum.

Computers and Their Potential Applications in Museums; *A Conference Sponsored by the Metropolitan Museum of Art, April 15, 16, and 17, 1968.* New York: Arno Press for the Metropolitan Museum, 1968. 402 pp., illus., bibliog. references.

Durand, Jacques. "The Use of Cultural and Scientific Films in the Museums of the World," *Museum,* XVI:2 (1963), pp. 102-114.

Fagaly, William; Gilbert Wright; and Frederick Dockstader. "Thoughts on the Audio-Visual Revolution," *Museum News,* 51:5 (January 1973), pp. 13-14. ◆ Three museum professionals register their feelings on the audiovisual revolution in exhibit technology.

Gilborn, Craig A. "Filmstrips and Slides," *Museum News,* 46:2 (October 1967), pp. 24-27. ◆ Discusses the use of films or slides to interpret visual material in terms of its cultural significance.

Haber, Franklin. "Reproducing the Arts Through Color Television," *Museum News,* 46:6 (February 1968), pp. 26-27.

Howard, James, and Sylvia Lanford Marchant. "Electragraphics," *Museum News,* 52:5 (January-February 1974), pp. 41-44. ◆ The rationale behind the development of a TV/video-tape production facility.

Katzive, David. "Museums Enter the Video Generation," *Museum News,* 51:5 (January 1973), pp. 20-24. ◆ A survey of how many museums own and use video equipment. Outlines some innovative uses of video equipment that can improve museum operations, programs and exhibits.

Kissiloff, William. "How to Use Mixed Media in Exhibits," *Curator,* XII:2 (June 1969), pp. 83-95.

Lawton, Sherman P. "Museum Television Programs: A Report on Practices," *Midwest Museums Conference Quarterly*, 17:3 (1957), pp. 30-47.

Lee, Robert S. "The Future of the Museum as a Learning Environment." In *Computers and Their Potential Applications in Museums* (New York: Arno Press, 1968), pp. 367-388. ◆ A report on the potential of the computer as a learning instrument in the museum environment, with emphasis on Montessori educational theory.

Libin, Laurence. "Two Sense Worth," *Museum News*, 52:5 (January-February 1974), pp. 50-52. ◆ Describes an audio-assisted gallery at the Metropolitan Museum of Art in which the musical instruments speak for themselves.

Lillys, William. "Museum TV: Its Genesis," *Museum News*, 51:5 (January 1973), pp. 15-19. ◆ Describes a program at the Boston Museum of Fine Arts. Urges other institutions to establish a nationwide network of televised museum programs.

McLuhan, Marshall. *Understanding Media: The Extensions of Man.* 2nd ed. New York: New American Library, 1973. 364 pp.

"McLuhanism in the Museum," *Museum News*, 46:7 (March 1968), pp. 11-18.

Mahaffey, Ben D. *Relative Effectiveness and Visitor Preference of Three Audio-Visual Media for Interpretation of an Historic Area.* College Station, Tex.: Texas A & M University, 1969. 63 pp., illus., bibliog., appendices.

Norgate, Martin. *Linked Tape and Slide Audio-Visual Displays.* London: Museums Association, 1973. 4 pp.

Radford, Thomas. "From A to V," *Museum News*, 52:5 (January-February 1974), pp. 36-40. ◆ Some considerations and guidelines on developing AV presentations for exhibitions, education, and outreach.

Rees, Matilda B., and William J. Paisley. *Social and Psychological Predictors of Information Seeking and Media Use, a Multivariate Re-Analysis.* Stanford, Calif.: Stanford University Institute for Communication Research, 1967. various pagings, bibliog. ◆ Photocopy available from ERIC Document Reproduction Service, Computer Microfilm International Corporation, P.O. Box 190, Arlington, Virginia 22210. ERIC # ED 017 819. A report on the use of the total communication system of society by adults. A pioneering study of selective use of different media. Of interest to museum personnel trying to determine where museums fit in the total system.

Ross, David A. "Search for Tomorrow," *Museum News*, 52:5 (January-February 1974), pp. 55-57. ◆ One alternative to the control of TV by a few corporate giants is museum development of programs for in-house and cable TV use.

Rushton, Brian H. "Producing and Selling a Quality Service to Education—Slides," *Museum News*, 46:5 (January 1968), pp. 27-32. ◆ The Tate Gallery's approach to the production of color slides.

Schoener, Allon. "The Electronic Museum and Information Distribution." In *Computers and Their Potential Applications in Museums* (New York: Arno Press, 1968), pp. 359-366. ◆ Discusses the shift in the philosophy of museum education from object recognition to information distribution and the role of the computer in this change.

Screven, Chandler G. "The Application of Programed Learning and Teaching Systems Procedures for Instruction in a Museum Environment." In *The Museum Visitor: Selected Essays and Surveys on Visitor Reaction to Exhibits in the Milwaukee Public Museum* (Milwaukee: Milwaukee Public Museum, 1968), pp. 167-174. ◆ Describes a project to adapt the basic features and methods of programed instruction and reinforcement theory to improve the instructional efficiency of museum exhibits.

Shannon, Joseph. "The Icing is Good, But the Cake is Rotten," *Museum News*, 52:5 (January-February 1974), pp. 28-35. ◆ The author decries the adulteration of museum exhibits with audio-visual technology.

Shettel, Harris H. "Exhibits: Art Form or Education Medium?" *Museum News*, 52:1 (September 1973), pp. 32-41.

Smith, Arthur L. "Producing the Slide Show for Your Historical Society," *History News*, 22:6 (June 1967), Technical Leaflet no. 42.

"Television Section: Production, Programming of Television," *Museum News*, 45:7 (March 1967), pp. 35-39. ◆ Includes: Patricia Barnard, "Problems and Techniques in Producing Museum Programs"; Curtis W. Davis, "Varieties in Programming."

Toker, Franklin K. B. "Slide Tapes for the Art Museum," *Museum News,* 47:1 (September 1968), Technical Supplement no. 24.

Tyrrell, William G. "Tape-Recording Local History," *History News,* 21:5 (May 1966), Technical Leaflet no. 35.

White, Stephen. "Implications of Technology for Museum Education." In *Museums and Education* (Washington, D.C.: Smithsonian Institution Press, 1968), pp. 193-203.

NOTES AND PERIODICALS

Association for Educational Communications and Technology, 1201 16th Street, N.W., Washington, D.C. 20036. An association of professionals responsible for the design and management of instructional materials in education and training. The functions of its membership are to apply processes and things to instruction; to process innovation, particularly instructional innovation; to develop alternatives to current practice. Publications: *A-V Communication Review,* a scholarly journal devoted to communication, technology and the teaching-learning process.

A-V Communication Review. 1953, quarterly, subscription. Association for Educational Communications and Technology, 1201 16th Street, N.W., Washington, D.C. 20036. ◆ A scholarly journal devoted to communication, technology and the teaching-learning process.

Media and Methods: Exploration in Education. 1965, monthly (September-May), subscription. North American Publishing Co., 134 North 13th Street, Philadelphia, Pennsylvania 19107. ◆ Devoted to visual learning with concentration on audiovisual aids and pictures. Excellent source for advertisements on commercially available media.

Media Techniques

Adams, Ansel E. *Artificial Light Photography.* Basic Photo Series, 5. Hastings-on-Hudson, N.Y.: Morgan & Morgan, 1968. 116 pp., illus.

Adams, Ansel E. *Camera and Lens, the Creative Approach: Studio, Laboratory, and Operation.* Basic Photo Series, 1. 1st rev. ed.

Hastings-on-Hudson, N.Y.: Morgan & Morgan, 1970. 304 pp., illus.

Adams, Ansel E. *Natural-Light Photography.* Basic Photo Series, 4. New rev. ed. Hastings-on-Hudson, N.Y.: Morgan & Morgan, 1969. 118 pp., illus.

Adams, Ansel E. *The Negative: Exposure and Development.* Basic Photo Series, 2. Hastings-on-Hudson, N.Y.: Morgan & Morgan, 1968. 120 pp., illus.

Adams, Ansel E. *The Print: Contact Printing and Enlarging.* Basic Photo Series, 3. New rev. ed. Hastings-on-Hudson, N.Y.: Morgan & Morgan, 1968. 120 pp., illus.

American Cinematographer Manual. 3rd ed. Compiled and edited by Arthur C. Miller and William Strenge. Hollywood: American Society of Cinematographers, 1969. 650 pp., illus.

Brown, James W.; Richard B. Lewis; and Fred F. Harcleroad. *A-V Instruction: Technology, Media and Methods.* 4th ed. New York: McGraw-Hill Book Co., 1973. 584 pp., illus., bibliog. ◆ Textbook on the characteristics and utilization of all types of audiovisual instructional materials and equipment. First and second editions titled: *A-V Instruction: Materials and Methods.* Third edition titled: *A-V Instruction: Media and Methods.*

Cable, Ralph. *Audiovisual Handbook.* 3rd ed. London: University of London Press, 1970. 118 pp., illus.

Eastman Kodak Company. *Audiovisual Planning Equipment.* Rochester, N.Y.: Eastman Kodak Co., 1974. 8 pp., illus.

Eastman Kodak Company. *Basic Copying.* Rochester, N.Y.: Eastman Kodak Co., 1973. 8 pp., illus.

Eastman Kodak Company. *Basic Magnetic Sound Recording for Motion Pictures.* 3rd ed. Rochester, N.Y.: Eastman Kodak Co., 1969. 41 pp., illus. ◆ Describes basic techniques, such as use of current equipment, script preparation, shooting for sound, recording sound and editing.

Eastman Kodak Company. *Basic Production Techniques for Motion Pictures.* Rochester, N.Y.: Eastman Kodak Co., 1971. 60 pp., illus., bibliog., glossary. ◆ Contains "how-to" information for business, industry, medicine, television, education and government.

Eastman Kodak Company. *Basic Titling and Animation for Motion Pictures.* Rochester, N.Y.: Eastman Kodak Co., 1972. 55 pp., bibliog., glossary. ◆ Methods for the small-scale producer of titles and/or animated films, such as teacher, trainer, etc.

Eastman Kodak Company. *Copying.* 8th ed. Rochester, N.Y.: Eastman Kodak Co., 1971. 32 pp., illus. ◆ Discusses lighting, exposure, processing; gives data on Kodak films for copying.

Eastman Kodak Company. *Effective Lecture Slides.* Rochester, N.Y.: Eastman Kodak Co., 1973. 4 pp., illus.

Eastman Kodak Company. *The Elephants of Visual Literacy.* Rochester, N.Y.: Eastman Kodak Co., 1972. 11 pp., illus. ◆ Defines visual literacy and visual communication and tells how photographic visuals can be created and interpreted.

Eastman Kodak Company. *Legibility— Artwork to Screen.* Rochester, N.Y.: Eastman Kodak Co., 1973. 8 pp., illus.

Eastman Kodak Company. *Making Black-and-White or Colored Transparencies for Overhead Projection (Using Kodak Products).* Rochester, N.Y.: Eastman Kodak Co., 1972. 4 pp.

Eastman Kodak Company. *Preparing Materials for Visual Presentations.* Rochester, N.Y.: Eastman Kodak Co., 1974. 10 pp., illus., sources of materials.

Eastman Kodak Company. *Producing Slides and Filmstrips.* 4th rev. ed. Rochester, N.Y.: Eastman Kodak Co., 1970. 55 pp., illus.

Eastman Kodak Company. *Projection Distance Tables for Kodak Ektagraphic and Carousel Slide Projectors.* Rochester, N.Y.: Eastman Kodak Co., 1974. 4 pp., illus.

Eastman Kodak Company. *Reflection Characteristics of Front-Projection Screen Materials.* Rochester, N.Y.: Eastman Kodak Co., 1972. 8 pp., illus.

Eastman Kodak Company. *Reverse-Text Slides from Black-on-White Line Artwork.* Rochester, N.Y.: Eastman Kodak Co., 1974. 8 pp.

Eastman Kodak Company. *Self-Contained Projection Cabinets.* Rochester, N.Y.: Eastman Kodak Co., 1972. 23 pp., illus., bibliog.

Eastman Kodak Company. *A Simple Wooden Copying Stand for Making Title Slides and Filmstrips.* Rochester, N.Y.: Eastman Kodak Co., 1973. 4 pp., illus.

Eastman Kodak Company. *Wide-Screen and Multiple-Screen Presentations.* Rochester, N.Y.: Eastman Kodak Co., 1973. 16 pp.

Eboch, Sidney C. *Operating Audiovisual Equipment.* 2nd ed. San Francisco: Chandler Publishing Co., 1968. 76 pp., illus., bibliog.

Herman, Lewis. *Educational Films: Writing, Directing, and Producing for Classroom, Television and Industry.* New York: Crown Publishers, 1965. 338 pp. ◆ Basic reference on principles, practices and techniques.

Kemp, Jerrold E., et al. *Planning and Producing Audiovisual Materials.* 2nd ed. San Francisco: Chandler Publishing Co., 1968. 251 pp., illus., bibliog. ◆ Includes planning audiovisual materials, fundamental skills (photography, graphics, sound recording), and producing materials (picture series, slides, filmstrips, transparencies, motion pictures, television).

Kinder, James S. *Using Instructional Media.* New York: Van Nostrand, 1973. 271 pp., illus., bibliog.

McMahan, Harry Wayne. *TV Tape Commercials: New Techniques of Creating and Producing Television Advertising.* New York: Hastings House, 1960. 110 pp., illus.

Matthews, Sydney K. *Photography in Archeology and Art.* New York: Humanities Press, 1968. 161 pp., illus., bibliog. ◆ For amateurs and professionals who wish to find new ways of presenting their photographs either for record, exhibition, or publicity purposes.

Mattingly, Grayson, and Welby Smith. *Introducing the Single-Camera VTR System: A Layman's Guide to Videotape Recording.* New York: Charles Scribner's Sons, 1973. 150 pp., illus.

"Media Report," *Museum News,* 1974-. ◆ A monthly column which is a compilation of news on films, videotape, cable and commercial TV programs about museums, AV technology and notes on publications of interest to the museum field.

Mees, Charles E. K. *The Theory of the Photographic Process.* 3rd ed. by T. H. James. New York: Macmillan, 1966. 591 pp., illus., bibliog. references.

Minor, Ed, and Harvey R. Frye. *Techniques for Producing Visual Instructional Media.* New York: McGraw-Hill Book Co., 1970. 305 pp., illus., annotated bibliog. ◆ Simplified methods for persons with and without skill in art, graphic arts and photography. Includes patterns and sketches for preparing visuals. Tells how to make transparencies, do lettering and printing and coloring techniques.

Norgate, Martin. *Linked Tape and Slide Audio-Visual Displays.* London: Museums Association, 1973. 4 pp.

Parker, Norton S. *Audiovisual Script Writing.* New Brunswick, N.J.: Rutgers University Press, 1968. 330 pp., illus. ◆ Intended for the beginning film writer—gives basic information about the audiovisual medium and the rudiments of the craft of scriptwriting, concluding with a checklist of twenty-six fundamentals.

Shulman, Julius. *Photographing Architecture and Interiors.* New York: Watson-Guptill, 1962. 154 pp., illus.

Smith, Arthur L. "Producing the Slide Show for Your Historical Society," *History News,* 22:6 (June 1967), Technical Leaflet no. 42.

Stasheff, Edward, and Rudy Bretz. *The Television Program: Its Direction and Production.* New York: Hill and Wang, 1968. 336 pp., illus.

Tall, Joel. *Techniques of Magnetic Tape Recording.* With Chapter Seven, "Recording Sound in Nature," by Peter Paul Kellogg. New York: Macmillan, 1958. 472 pp., illus., bibliog.

Texas, University. Visual Instruction Bureau. *Production of 2 x 2 Inch Slides for School Use.* Prepared by Joe Coltharp. Austin, Tex.: University of Texas, 1970. 79 pp., illus., bibliog.

Tyrrell, William G. "Tape-Recording Local History," *History News,* 21:5 (May 1966), Technical Leaflet no. 35..

Videofreex (organization). *The Spaghetti City Video Manual: A Guide to Use, Repair and Maintenance.* New York: Praeger, 1973. 116 pp., illus., bibliog.

Wittich, Walter Arno, and Charles Francis

Schuller, eds. *Instructional Technology: Its Nature and Use.* 5th ed. New York: Harper & Bros., 1973. 554 pp. ◆ A comprehensive and scholarly treatment of audiovisual materials and their use. Includes discussion of motion pictures, educational television, language laboratories, and programmed learning.

Zettl, Herbert. *Television Production Handbook.* 2nd ed. Belmont, Calif.: Wadsworth Publishing Co., 1968. 448 pp. ◆ Complete reference work on all phases of TV production.

NOTES AND PERIODICALS

Afterimage. 1972, monthly, subscription, tabloid format. Visual Studies Workshop, 4 Elton Street, Rochester, New York 14607.

Audio-Visual Communications. 1961, 9 issues per year, subscription. United Business Publications, Inc., 200 Madison Avenue, New York, New York, 10016. Formerly: *Film Audio-Visual Communications.*

Audiovisual Institute for Effective Communication, Indiana University, Bloomington, Indiana 47401. The Institute, sponsored by the National Audio-Visual Association, is a five day course of comprehensive audiovisual instruction with a faculty of nationally known audiovisual instruction specialists. It is open to anyone who needs specialized media training. Sessions include general lectures on media and special workshops on videotape, motion picture production, slide and filmstrip production, multi-media presentations. For more information contact: National Audio-Visual Association, 3150 Spring Street, Fairfax, Virginia 22030.

Audiovisual Instruction. 1956, monthly (September-June), subscription. Department of Audiovisual Instruction, National Education Association and Association for Educational Communications and Technology, 1201 16th Street, N.W., Washington, D.C. 20006. ◆ News, notes and articles geared to provide authoritative help for school administrators, supervisors, building coordinators and audiovisual specialists.

Audiovisual Notes. 1970, two issues per year, subscription. Eastman Kodak Company, 343 State Street, Rochester, New York 14650.

Image. Journal of Photography of the George Eastman House. 1952, 10 issues per year, membership. George Eastman House Associates, 900 East Avenue, Rochester, New York 14650.

Index to Kodak Information, published once a year, lists all Eastman Kodak publications. Eastman Kodak Company, 343 State Street, Rochester, New York 14650.

NAVA. 1946, fortnightly, subscription. National Audio-Visual Association, 3150 Spring Street, Fairfax, Virginia 22030.

Picturescope. 1953, quarterly, subscription. New York Public Library, Picture Collections, Fifth Avenue at 42nd Street, New York, New York 10018.

Administering Instructional Media Programs

Brown, James Wilson; Kenneth D. Norberg; and Sara K. Srygley. *Administering Educational Media: Instructional Technology and Library Services.* 2nd ed. New York: McGraw-Hill Book Co., 1972. 449 pp., illus., bibliog.

Erickson, Carlton W. H. *Administering Instructional Media Programs.* New York: Macmillan Publishing Co., 1968. 660 pp., illus., bibliog. ◆ Beginning with the nature of the media program director's job, this book covers the acquisition, distribution, physical facilities and service system within the individual program. One chapter is devoted to organizing a city-wide audiovisual media center.

St. Louis, Charles, and Thomas G. Lee. *Administering an Instructional Film Program: A Handbook for the Building Audiovisual Coordinator.* Muskegon, Mich.: Instructional Media Services, Mona Shores Schools, 1970. 40 pp., illus. ◆ Includes examples of forms, letters, memos, and checklists used for ordering, booking, student assistants, etc. Instructional Media Services, 3429 Henry Street, Muskegon, Michigan 49441.

Sources of Audiovisual Materials and Equipment

Chedister, Ron. "You Have to Shop Around," *Museum News,* 52:5 (January-February 1974), pp. 63-64.

Clapp, Jane. *Art Reproductions.* New York: The Scarecrow Press, 1961. 350 pp. ◆ Reproductions available from ninety-five museums in the United States and Canada.

Eastman Kodak Company. *Motion Picture and AV Publications: Selected References.* Rochester, N.Y.: Eastman Kodak Company, 1972. 26 pp.

Eastman Kodak Company. *Some Sources of 2 x 2 Color Slides.* Rochester, N.Y.: Eastman Kodak Company, 1972. 11 pp.

Eastman Kodak Company. *Sources of Motion Pictures and Filmstrips.* Rochester, N.Y.: Eastman Kodak Co., 1972. 22 pp.

Eastman Kodak Company. *Sources of Motion Picture Services and Equipment—16mm, 8mm and Super 8.* Rochester, N.Y.: Eastman Kodak Company, 1972. 6 pp.

Eastman Kodak Company. *Sources of Super 8 Film in Kodak Supermatic Cassettes.* Rochester, N.Y.: Eastman Kodak Co., 1974. 16 pp., illus.

Educational Media Council. *Educational Media Index. A Project of the Educational Media Council.* New York: McGraw-Hill Book Co., 1964. 14 vols. ◆ Individual volumes available separately. Lists educational motion pictures, filmstrips, kinescopes, charts, graphs, maps in sets, cross-media kits, flat pictures in sets, models, mock-ups, phonodiscs, phonotapes, programed instructional materials, slides, transparencies, and videotapes available for educational use anywhere in the U.S.

Gidley, M. A. *Audio-Visual Materials for American Studies: A Guide to Sources of Information and Materials.* Exeter, Eng.: American Arts Documentation Center, 1972. 105 pp.

Kelley, Winslow, and Thomas J. Serb. *Audio-Visual Aids and Equipment.* Chicago: American Society of Planning Officials, 1962. 62 pp., illus.

Laird, Dugan. *A User's Look at the Audio-Visual World.* 2nd ed. Fairfax, Va.: National Audio-Visual Association, Inc., 1974. 47 pp., illus., bibliog. ◆ Answers most commonly asked questions about selecting vendors and equipment, performance standards, etc. Also provides detailed information on sound projection and viewers, filmstrip equipment, slide and other projectors, learning laboratory systems, AV furniture.

Moorachian, Rose. *What is a City? A Multi-Media Guide on Urban Living.* Boston: Boston Public Library, 1969. 152 pp., illus. ♦ Bibliography of books, tapes, films and other learning resources for young people on aspects of urban life.

Morlan, John E. *Preparation of Inexpensive Teaching Materials.* 2nd ed. New York: Chandler Publishing Co., 1973. 180 pp., illus., bibliog., materials sources.

National Audiovisual Center. National Archives and Records Service. *A Catalog of United States Government Produced Audiovisual Materials.* Washington, D.C.: National Audiovisual Center, National Archives and Records Service, General Services Administration, 1974. 356 pp. ♦ Entries listed by title and by subject.

Petrini, Sharon, and Troy-John Bromberger. *A Handlist of Museum Sources for Slides and Photographs.* Santa Barbara, Calif.: Slide Library, Art Department, University of California, 1972. 147 pp.

Rufsvold, Margaret I., and Carolyn Guss. *Guides to Educational Media; Films, Filmstrips, Kinescopes, Phonodiscs, Phonotapes, Programed Instruction Materials, Slides, Transparencies and Videotapes.* 3rd ed. Chicago: American Library Association, 1971. 116 pp. ♦ An annotated, comprehensive guide which identifies and describes catalogs and lists services of professional organizations and specialized periodicals which systematically provide information on educational media.

Special Libraries Association. Picture Division. *Picture Sources 3.* New York: The Association, 1975. 387 pp., indexes. ♦ Directory to collections of prints and photographs in U.S. and Canada. Includes an alphabetical list of sources and geographical list of sources.

Wasserman, Paul, ed. *Museum Media: A Biennial Directory and Index of Publications and Audiovisuals Available from United States and Canadian Institutions.* Detroit: Gale Research Co., 1973. 455 pp. ♦ Intended to provide bibliographic control of books, booklets, monographs, catalogs, pamphlets and leaflets, films and filmstrips, and other media which are prepared and distributed by

museums, art galleries and related institutions in the United States and Canada. Biennial publication is planned.

Wonderly, Robert, and Charles Van Horn. "Keep in Touch," *Museum News,* 52:5 (January-February 1974), pp. 65-66. Describes two national associations that provide informational and educational services on A-V technology.

Zeitlin, Stanley S. "Something for Nothing," *Museum News,* 52:5 (January-February 1974), pp. 53-54. ♦ A guide to obtaining fine films on a free loan basis from major corporations.

NOTES AND PERIODICALS

American Library Color Slide Company, Inc., 305 East 45th Street, New York, New York 10017.

Audiovisual Instruction. 1956, monthly (September-June), subscription. Department of Audiovisual Instruction, National Education Association for Educational Communications and Technology, 1201 16th Street, N.W., Washington, D.C. 20006.

Audiovisual Marketplace; A Multimedia Guide. 1969, biennial. R. R. Bowker Co., P.O. Box 1807, Ann Arbor, Michigan 48106.

The Blue Book of Audio-Visual Materials. Published annually in the August issue of *Educational Screen and Audiovisual Guide.* Educational Screen and Audiovisual Guide, 434 South Wabash Street, Chicago, Illinois 60605. ♦ A descriptive list of over 700 films, filmstrips, slide sets, maps, classroom recordings, and non-projected teaching tools for education, industry, entertainment, and community purposes.

BY-WORD, Educational Service Programs, Inc., 557 Columbus Avenue, New Haven, Connecticut 06519. BY-WORD consists of lightweight headsets that require no wires or other attachments. They are tuned to pick up a magnetic field around each display at the museum. As the visitor walks into the field, the taped narrative is transmitted to the earphones.

Commercial Slides Committee, College Art Association Slide and Photograph Librarians, *A Slide Buyer's Guide.* Available from Curator of Slides and Photographs, Department of Art and History, University of Missouri-Kansas City, Kansas City, Missouri 64110.

Consumer Reports should be consulted for the most recent product testing reports on audiovisual equipment. Consumer's Union of U.S., Inc., 256 Washington Street, Mount Vernon, New York 10550.

Eastman Kodak Co. *Index to Kodak Information,* published once a year, lists all Eastman Kodak publications.

Educational Media Council, Inc., 1346 Connecticut Avenue, N.W., Washington, D.C. 20036. The members of the Educational Media Council are nonprofit national associations or organizations having a substantial concern with educational media and materials. It serves its members as a forum for discussion of developments and problems of mutual concern and as an information clearinghouse. The Council undertakes research and dissemination projects which by their nature and scope are beyond the capacity of individual member organizations and which are deemed serviceable to member constituencies and the educational community at large.

Educational Screen and Audiovisual Guide. 1922, monthly, subscription. Trade Periodicals, Inc., 434 South Wabash Avenue, Chicago, Illinois 60605. ◆ Includes systematic evaluations of new films, filmstrips, recordings and descriptions of new products.

Educators Guide to Free Films. 1941, annual. Educators Progress Service, Randolph, Wisconsin 53956. ◆ Annotated list by title, subject and source.

Educators Guide to Free Filmstrips. 1949, annual. Educators Progress Service, Inc., Randolph, Wisconsin 53956. ◆ Annotated list by title, subject and source.

Educators Guide to Free Social Studies Materials. 1961, annual. Educators Progress Service, Randolph, Wisconsin 53956. ◆ Lists generally available free and free loan educational and informational social studies films, filmstrips, sets of slides, tapes, scripts, phono records and other supplementary materials

such as bulletins, pamphlets, exhibits, charts, posters and books.

Media and Methods: Exploration in Education. 1965, monthly (September-May), subscription. North American Publishing Co., 134 North 13th Street, Philadelphia, Pennsylvania 19107. ◆ Devoted to visual learning with concentration on audiovisual aids and motion pictures. Excellent source for advertisements on commercially available media.

Modern Photography. 1937, monthly, subscription. Herbert Keppler, 165 West 46th Street, New York, New York 10036. ◆ Good source for advertisements for audiovisual equipment.

National Audio-Visual Association (NAVA), 3150 Spring Street, Fairfax, Virginia 22030. The national trade association of the commercial A-V industry. Membership consists of dealers, rental libraries, manufacturers of A-V equipment and materials, film producers and producers of other A-V materials, publishers, independent audio-visual representatives and A-V professional services members. The Association sponsors seminars, institutes and publishes a membership directory. Publications include a biweekly newsletter, *Audio-Visual Equipment Directory,* and *A User's Look at the Audio-Visual World.*

National Park Service Audiovisual Productions, Harpers Ferry Historical Association, P.O. Box 147, Harpers Ferry, West Virginia 25425. Harpers Ferry Historical Association has been designated distributing agent for audiovisual productions of the National Park Service. National Park Service films will now be available on a nationwide basis through both sales and rental by this authorized agent. Harpers Ferry Historical Association, a Park Service affiliated cooperating association, operates the National Park Service bookstore in Harpers Ferry, in addition to being distributing agency and central booking office for films.

Popular Photography. 1937, monthly, subscription. Ziff-Davis Publishing Co., Box 1097, Flushing, New York 11352. ◆ Good source for advertisements for audiovisual equipment.

APPENDIX

Periodicals Cited

Afterimage. 1972, monthly, subscription, tabloid format. Visual Studies Workshop, 4 Elton Street, Rochester, New York 14607.

The American Archivist. 1938, quarterly, subscription. Society of American Archivists, Box 8198, University of Illinois at Chicago Circle, Chicago, Illinois 60680.

American Education. 1965, monthly (January-February and August-September combined), subscription. Superintendent of Documents, U.S. Government Printing Office, Washington, D.C. 20402.

American Journal of Public Health and the Nation's Health. 1911, monthly, subscription. American Public Health Association, 1740 Broadway, New York, New York 10019.

Audio-Visual Communications. 1961, 9 issues per year, subscription. United Business Publications, Inc., 200 Madison Avenue, New York, New York 10016.

Audiovisual Instruction. 1956, monthly (September-June), subscription. Department of Audiovisual Instruction, National Education Association and Association for Educational Communications and Technology, 1201 16th Street, N.W., Washington, D.C. 20006.

Audiovisual Notes. 1970, two issues per year, subscription. Eastman Kodak Co., 343 State Street, Rochester, New York 14650.

A-V Communication Review. 1953, quarterly, subscription. Association for Educational Communications and Technology, 1201 16th Street, N.W., Washington, D.C. 20036.

Bicentennial Bulletin. 1971, weekly, free. American Revolution Bicentennial Administration, 2401 E Street, N.W., Washington, D.C. 20276.

Bicentennial Times. 1974, monthly, free. American Revolution Bicentennial Administra-

tion, 2401 E Street, N.W., Washington, D.C. 20276.

(CMA) Gazette/(AMC) Gazette. 1966, six issues per year, subscription. Canadian Museums Association, 331 Cooper Street, Suite 400, Ottawa, Ontario, K2P 0G5.

Common Sense. 1973, bimonthly, subscription. People's Bicentennial Commission, 1346 Connecticut Avenue, N.W., Room 1025, Washington, D.C. 20036.

Consumer Reports. 1936, monthly, subscription. Consumer's Union of U.S., Inc., 256 Washington Street, Mount Vernon, New York 10550.

Curator. 1958, quarterly, subscription. American Museum of Natural History, 79th Street at Central Park West, New York, New York 10024.

Design Quarterly. 1946, four issues per year, subscription. Walker Art Center, 807 Hennepin Avenue, Minneapolis, Minnesota 55403.

Discovery. 1968, quarterly, membership. Association for the Preservation of Virginia Antiquities, 2705 Park Avenue, Richmond, Virginia 23220.

Educational Leadership. 1943, monthly (October-May), subscription. Association for Supervision and Curriculum, 1201 16th Street, N.W., Washington, D.C. 20036.

Educational Screen and Audiovisual Guide. 1922, monthly, subscription. Trade Periodicals, Inc., 434 South Wabash Avenue, Chicago, Illinois 60605.

Educational Technology. 1961, monthly, subscription. Educational Technology Publications, Inc., 140 Sylvan Avenue, Englewood Cliffs, New Jersey 17632.

Environment Southwest. 1967, monthly, subscription or membership. San Diego Natural History Museum, P.O. Box 501, San Diego, California 92112.

Guideline. 1971, bimonthly, subscription. National Conference on State Parks, Park Practice Program, 1601 North Kent Street, Arlington, Virginia 22209.

Historic Preservation. 1949, quarterly, membership. National Trust for Historic Preservation, 740-748 Jackson Place, N.W., Washington, D.C. 20006.

History News. 1941, monthly, membership. American Association for State and Local History, 1400 Eighth Avenue South, Nashville, Tennessee 37203.

(ICOM) Museums' Annual: Education–Cultural Action. 1969, annual, subscription. ICOM Secretariat, Maison de l'UNESCO, 1 Rue Miollis, 75732, Paris, France. New title— *ICOM Education* beginning with No. 7, 1975/1976 double issue.

ICOM News. 1948, quarterly, membership or subscription. International Council of Museums, 1 Rue Miollis, 75732, Paris, France.

Image. Journal of Photography of the George Eastman House. 1952, ten issues per year, membership. George Eastman House Associates, 900 East Avenue, Rochester, New York 14650.

Industrial Design; Designing for Industry. 1954, ten issues per year, subscription. Whitney Publications, Inc., 130 East 59th Street, New York, New York 10022.

Interiors. 1888, monthly, subscription. Whitney Publications, Inc., 130 East 59th Street, New York, New York 10022.

International Lighting Review. 1950, quarterly, subscription. Foundation "Prometheus," NZ Voorburgwal 271-273, Amsterdam C, Netherlands.

Journal of World History. 1953-1972, quarterly, subscription. Unipub, Box 433, 650 First Avenue, New York, New York 10016. Superseded by *Cultures*.

Living Historical Farms Bulletin. 1970, quarterly, membership. Association for Living Historical Farms and Agricultural Museums, Smithsonian Institution, Washington, D.C. 20560.

Media and Methods: Exploration in Educa-

tion. 1965, monthly (September-May), subscription. North American Publishing Co., 134 North 13th Street, Philadelphia, Pennsylvania 19107.

Midwest Museums Conference Quarterly. 1941, quarterly, membership. Grand Rapids Public Museum, 54 Jefferson Avenue, S.E., Grand Rapids, Michigan 49502. Midwest regional conference of the American Association of Museums.

Midwest Region Interpretive Newsletter. 1973, quarterly, membership. National Park Service, Midwest Regional Office, 1709 Jackson Street, Omaha, Nebraska 68102.

Modern Photography. 1937, monthly, subscription. Herbert Keppler, 165 West 46th Street, New York, New York 10036.

The Museologist. 1935, quarterly, membership. Buffalo and Erie County Historical Society, 25 Nottingham Court, Buffalo, New York 14216. Northeast Conference of Museums of the American Association of Museums.

Museum. 1948, quarterly, subscription. UNESCO Publications Center, 801 Third Avenue, New York, New York 10022.

Museum News, 1924, six issues per year, membership or subscription. American Association of Museums, 1055 Thomas Jefferson Street, N.W., Washington, D.C. 20007.

Museums Journal. 1901, quarterly, membership or subscription. The Museums Association, 87 Charlotte Street, London WC1, England.

NAVA. 1946, fortnightly, subscription. National Audio-Visual Association, 3150 Spring Street, Fairfax, Virginia 22030.

New York State Education. 1914, monthly (October-May), membership. New York State Teacher's Association, 152 Washington Avenue, Albany, New York 12210.

New York Times Magazine (section of New York Times Sunday edition). New York Times Co., 229 West 43rd Street, New York, New York 10036.

Picturescope. 1953, quarterly, subscription. New York Public Library, Picture Collections, Fifth Avenue at 42nd Street, New York, New York 10018.

Planning and Civic Comment. 1935-1965, quarterly. National Conference on State Parks, 1601 North Kent Street, Arlington, Virginia 22209.

Popular Photography. 1937, monthly, subscription. Ziff-Davis Publishing Co., 1 Park Ave., New York, N.Y. 10016.

Reader's Digest. 1922, monthly, subscription. Reader's Digest Association, Inc., Pleasantville, New York 10570.

Research in Education. 1966, monthly, subscription. U.S. Government Printing Office, Washington, D.C. 20405.

Social Education. 1937, monthly (October-May), membership or subscription. National Council for the Social Studies, 1201 16th Street, N.W., Washington, D.C. 20036.

Studies in Conservation. 1952, quarterly, membership or subscription. International Institute for Conservation of Historic and Artistic Works, 6 Buckingham St., London WC2N 6BA, England.

Technical Studies in the Field of Fine Arts. 1932-1942, monthly. William Hayes Fogg Art Museum, Harvard University, Cambridge, Massachusetts 01438.

Technology and Culture: Devoted to the Study of the Development of Technology and Its Relations with Society and Culture. 1960, quarterly, subscription. University of Chicago Press, 5750 Ellis Avenue, Chicago, Illinois 60637.

Trans-Action—Social Science and Modern Society; to further the understanding and use of the social sciences. 1963, monthly, subscription. Rutgers University, New Brunswick, New Jersey 08903.

Trends. Vol. 5, 1968, quarterly, subscription. National Recreation and Park Association, Park Practice Program, 1601 N. Kent Street, Arlington, Virginia 22209. Formerly Trends in Parks and Recreation.

USA 200: The American Bicentennial Monthly. 1971, monthly, subscription. Bicentennial Council of the Thirteen Original States, c/o Brian Dow, Suite 2001, 400 Colony Square, Atlanta, Georgia 30361.

Visual Merchandising. 1922, monthly, subscription. Display Publishing Company, 407 Gilbert Avenue, Cincinnati, Ohio 45202. Formerly Display World.

The Yorker. 1942, 4 times per year, membership. New York State Historical Association, Cooperstown, New York 13326.

Index